AF553904

PROGRAMMED LEARNING

PREFACE

The objectives for publication of this book are to provide an introduction to the process of programmed learning in the discipline of education, and to provide reference material to the students who are pursuing their B.Ed., M.Ed and research courses in the said discipline. An attempt has been made to acquaint the students with the various stages through which the programmes in this study were prepared concerning topics related with Home Science with a focus on Food and Nutrition.

Programmed Learning is a branch of Educational Technology which stresses that a teacher be more objective and scientific in his/her approach towards teaching. Thus this book would prove to be extremely helpful to inservice teachers in generating interest in their students regarding the subject matter.

This book is based on a prolonged experimental research conducted through the responses of the twelfth grade students studying Home Science. Special care was taken by the author to make it interesting and lucid in style and composition. It depicts the originality of the author who was awarded a Ph.D. on its basis. This book would go a long way in helping both the teachers and the researchers in making innovations in Educational Technology. It is recommended for B.Ed., M.Ed., and students pursuing their research in Education, as it conforms to the courses prescribed for the said degrees in various universities and pedagogical colleges.

CONTENTS

Chapter 1

INTRODUCTION

In the present world, there is a growing respect for the scientific method as the chief method of intellectual inquiry. There seems very little to which the scientific method cannot be fruitfully applied. The notion of a scientific base for education is not new, but the strengthening of the scientific milieu in which this idea is now resurrected gives it particular conviction and popularity. The approach has given rise to emergence of technology in general scientific endeavours and education technology in the field of education.

Educational Technology has two meanings–hardware technology and software technology. Software technology refers to the detailed application of the psychology of learning to practical teaching problems. The educational technologist believes that he can build in the student a complex repertory of knowledge or behaviour by applying a few basic principles of learning psychology in addition to a little art of intuition. Hardware technology refers to the application of engineering principles in the development of electro mechanical equipment used for instructional purposes. Examples of these vices are motion pictures, tape recorders, teaching machines and computers. Software technology includes Programmed Instruction.

PART A

1. Concept of Programmed Learning

Programmed learning is the first systematic application of experimentally studied principles of behaviour control to the practical issues of education. It is used as a method to improve the teaching learning process. It is an individualized technique of instruction, in which the student is guided to participate actively by continually making responses.

Programmed learning is a systematic empirical attempt to convert the craft of teaching into a prescriptive theory and practice of instruction. Some popular definitions of programmed learning proposed by the experts of programming are in the proceeding discussion.

Smith and Moore (1962) defined programmed instruction as the process of arranging the material to be learnt into a series of sequential steps; usually it moves the student from a familiar background into a complex and new set of concepts, principles and understandings.

Green (1963) wrote the following statement, while expressing his own conception about programming : "A programme consists of a series of stimuli designed to exert increasing control over gradually developing behavioural repertory. Reinforcement derived from matching behaviour to the stimulus requirements accomplishes the differentiation procedure. The frames of the programme are discriminative stimuli anticipating probable courses of action on the part of the student and directing his actions by limiting the range of alternatives available to him. They are instructions in the broadest sense. Violating the limits results in non-reinforcement. Remaining within the bounds results in reinforcement. The bounds narrow progressively to define the ultimate form of the new repertory. As they have been developed, programmes make use of continuous reinforcement, both in the development of discrimination with regard to the material to be taught and in the differentiation of the response class to be shaped. In this respect programmes embody the means for rapid training. They also open possibilities for applying other techniques of control to produce more permanent learning."

Jacobs, Maier and Stolurow (1966) express that self instructional programmes are educational materials from which students learn. These programmes can be used with many types of students and subject matters, either by themselves, hence, the name "self-instruction" or in combination with other instructional techniques. The teaching technique based on self-instructional programmes is called self-instruction. Students can master the material without the aid of a live-instructor, so sometimes programmed instruction is also termed as auto-instruction. All self-instructional programmes have certain features in common. First, these require the student to focus his attention on a limited amount of material at one time. Second, these require him to respond in some way to each segment of material. Third, these give him immediate knowledge of results after every response. These three features in sequence, constitute what is called learning cycle, which is repeated many times in the program. Fourth, these permit each student to work at his own pace. Programmes may be presented on paper for reading, on tapes and records for listening, or on television and films for watching. All these features listed by Jacobs, Maier and Stolurow are to be found in programmes.

The most commonly held view of programmed instruction is the one derived from Skinner's work. This view as stated by Leith (1967) is that a programme is a sequence of small steps of instructional material (called frames), most of which require a response to be made by completing a blank space in a sentence. To ensure that expected responses are given, a system of cuing is applied, and each response is verified by the provision of immediate knowledge of results. Such a sequence is intended to be worked at the learner's own pace as individual self-instruction.

Susan Markle (1969) an expert in programmed learning defined it, as follows :

"It is a method of designing a reproducible sequence of instructional events to produce a measurable and consistent effect on behaviour of each and every acceptable student."

The above mentioned ideas reveal that Programmed Instruction is a technique of converting the live instructional process into self learning or auto-instructional readable material in the form of small segments which the learners are required to read, make some right or wrong response, correct wrong responses or confirm the right response and attain the complete mastery of the concepts explained in the micro sequences. These micro sequences called Frames, form a complex subject matter of some wider instructional sequence for a unit of instruction.

2. Origin of Programmed Learning

Programmed instruction is the outcome of research conducted by some experimental psychologists like Thorndike, Watson, Pavlov and Skinner, technically labelled as 'behaviourists.' The psychologists like Watson and Pavlov contributed indirectly to the movement of programmed instruction, in a sense, that they made human behaviour, especially the process of learning accessible to scientific investigation. Thorndike, is the first psychologist whose findings bear direct relevance to programmed learning. By 1954, Skinner developed a theory of learning called "Operant conditioning" which is applied in programmed learning.

Thorndike's law of effect has a relationship with programmed learning. Thorndike made a study of cats in a problem box. A hungry cat was confined in a cage with tempting morsel of fish outside. The cat could open the door by pulling a loop of string hanging inside the cage. The cat could open the door by successive trials. The improvement was very gradual. Even after several experiences of opening the door by pulling the string, animals on a given trial could still spend considerable time in other behaviour before pulling the string. This led Thorndike to conclude that the cat's learning to pull the string involved a gradual "stamping in" of the stimulus response connection between seeing the string and pulling it.

Thorndike's primary law of learning is the Law of Effect. This states that the "stamping in" of stimulus response connection depends not simply on the fact that the stimulus and response occur together but on the effects that follow the response. If a stimulus is followed by a response and then by a satisfier, stimulus response connection is strengthened. If however, a stimulus is followed by a response and then by an annoyance, the stimulus response connection is weakened. Thus, satisfying and annoying effects of responses determine whether the stimulus response connections are to be "stamped in" or "stamped out". So, according to Thorndike reward strengthens connection. In programmed learning, when the student is able to answer on the programme frame he is given rewards in the form of correction of the "Knowledge of Results."

Programmed Learning is related with the findings of Thorndike as the instructional technology uses the device called teaching machine which presents finally graded series of problems and provides immediate reinforcement for the learner's correct response.

Psychologists, like Watson and Pavlov contributed indirectly to the movement of Programmed Instruction. They accorded psychology the status of science and thus, made human behaviour, especially the process of learning, accessible to scientific investigation. The concept of psychology according to Watson is that, "Psychology as the behaviourist views it is purely objective experimental branch of natural science. Its theoretical goal is the prediction and control of behaviour." So, the experimental psychology sowed the seeds of Behaviourism which has a direct bearing on the movement of programmed learning.

Sydney L. Pressey (1927) is often credited with the widespread use of teaching device in the classroom. Initially Pressey was interested in an automatic testing device. He soon discovered that students could also learn by taking tests via his machine. Basically the type of device developed by Pressey followed the format of multiple choice items. The student was presented with a question and four options, only one of which was correct. The student chose an option and the device provided an immediate feed-back. If the learner chose the correct answer, the machine presented the next item, if an incorrect option was chosen by him, he continued responding till he selected the correct option. Pressey discovered that the machine not only saved a vast amount of marking time but also produced measurable increase in learning. He developed several models of recording devices. In this way Pressey paved the way for the development of instructional programmes which could be fed into the teaching machines. Also the need for empirically developed programmes was felt when the markets in United States started selling teaching machines along with other educational aids like films, tape recorders and overhead projectors. Thus, origin of the technique of programmed learning is essentially new and may be thought to have emerged from dynamic effort of American Psychologists during the second decade of the twentieth century.

In 1954, B. F. Skinner announced and embarked upon a series of investigations and inventions designed to increase the efficiency of teaching arithmetic, reading, spelling and other school subjects, by using a mechanical device expected to do some things much better than the usual teacher can do them while saving the teacher for tasks that the teacher can do better. An early form of the device presented number combinations for the teaching of addition. The child punches his answer in a kind of adding machine key board, if he answers correctly the machine moves on the next problem and "reinforcement" occurs.

Skinner's contribution to programmed learning is immense. He produced some of the first programs and teaching machines. Skinner's concern was with continuous and immediate reinforcement. This identifies him with traditional learning psychology. Even the programming technique has its traditional aspect. The use of rewards in learning, is not entirely a novel idea. Skinner uses the language of operant conditioning in describing the learning process. He gives a great importance to reinforcement and this leads him to emphasize the use of machines.

Operant conditioning is the learning process whereby a response is made more probable or more frequent. Skinner recognizes two different kinds of learning. They are different because each involves a separate kind of behaviour. Respondent behaviour is elicited by specific stimuli. Given the stimulus, the response occurs automatically. The knee jerk reflex is an example.

Skinner maintains however that most behaviour is of a different sort. This kind he refers to as OPERANT BEHAVIOUR. Whereas the distinctive characteristic of respondent behaviour is that it is in response to a stimuli, the characteristic of operant behaviour is that it operates on the environment. There is no particular stimulus that will consistently elicit an operant response. According to Skinner Operant behaviour is emitted by the organism rather than elicited by stimuli.

Skinner does not mean to say that operant behaviour is not influenced by stimuli. Much of his analysis of behaviour is concerned with ways in which operant behaviour is brought under the control of stimuli. However, such control is only partial and conditional. The operant response for reaching for food is not simply elicited by the sight of food, it also depends on hunger, social circumstances and variety of other stimulus conditions. In these respects, it is in contrast to the respondent knee-jerk response which is regularly elicited by a tap on the knee almost without regard to other conditions.

The learning of operant behaviour is also, known as conditioning, but it is different from the conditioning of reflexes. Operant conditioning is the same sort of learning that Thorndike described. If an operant response occurs and is followed by reinforcement it's probability of occurring again increases. Whereas for reflexes the reinforcer is an unconditioned stimulus for operants it is a reward. Thus, reward following an operant makes that response more likely to occur again.

Skinner formulated the theory of "Operant Conditioning" on the basis of extensive research carried on pigeons and rats. Skinner demonstrated that pigeons can be taught to perform surprising feats provided they are trained in very small steps taken one at a time and provided that each successful step is reinforced or rewarded. "If pigeon can be taught this way, so can be children" says, Skinner. The technique is to arrange and organize the complex subject matter into very small pieces of information, that can be learned step by step, and to reinforce success at each step by immediately telling the learner that the response is correct. By means of this technique the learner is lead in a series of easy and small steps. According to Skinner, the learner's verbal behaviour is 'shaped' through programmed instructional material. By harnessing, the principles of operant conditioning in teaching the human beings, Skinner developed some programmes and also evolved a teaching machine which circumvent the limitations of Pressey's model. Skinner evolved a sound auto-instructional model which is popularly known as Skinnerian or linear model of programming.

Programmed Instruction, today has evolved to a fine extent and is considered as a very important aspect of Educational Technology today. It started from experimental psychology and experimental study pertaining to the learning process by behaviourists. Today programmed instruction is an important aspect of the promising and exciting era of Educational Technology.

3. Basic Principles of Programmed Learning

Programmed Learning is the first application of the laboratory techniques utilized in the study of the learning process to the practical problems of education.

1. The first principle of programmed learning *is the principle of small steps*:- The basic idea of programmed learning is that the most efficient, pleasant and permanent learning takes place when the student proceeds through a course by large number of small, easy to take steps. Since the students have to grasp a little at a time, they are able to master the subject while making a few errors only.
2. The second principle of programmed learning is that of *active responding.* From the studies conducted by psychologists it has been proved that the student learns best if he is actively responding as he is learning. The learner remains busy and active when he is going through a programme. The learner can move to the next frame only if he has a thorough understanding of the previous frame. Active responding on the part of the learner means his involvement in the learning process. Active responding does not mean a small response to a small bit of information. The material of the programme is so structured that the learner is called

upon to make a series of responses to a series of frames. In some programmes, he cannot move ahead until he has correctly responded to the previous frame.

3. The third principle of programmed learning is the *principle of immediate confirmation.* A student learns best when he can confirm his response to a frame immediately. A student whose test is scored and made known immediately learns better than a student who has to wait for weeks for the result. Through the programme, the learner receives immediate confirmation of the correctness of his response before he proceeds to the next step. This reinforces the learning process. The principle of immediate confirmation is of great importance in the learning process. The learner will not wildly guess the responses, as he knows that his answers will be confirmed immediately. Also, if the learner is unsure of his response, he needs its confirmation. So, in programming the student can find out immediately if his answer is correct or incorrect.

4. The fourth basic principle of programmed learning is *self-pacing* : Every individual does not have the same pace of learning. Programmed learning, provides freedom to the learner to make fast or slow progress according to his own pace of learning. Thus, it keeps in mind the psychology of individual differences. Each learner proceeds with the programme at his own pace. The learner is not required to wait for those who are slower than him, nor is he required to rush through the programme if he is a slow learner. The student can take as much time as he wishes to work on a program.

5. The fifth basic principle of programmed learning is the *principle of student testing.* After every programme is conducted, a detailed record of the responses which have been made by the students is made and this

provides the basis for revising the programmes. Students may find some frames as too big or unclear. By looking at the programme, the programmer, can see exactly what steps can come before a particular step to make that step clearer. Detailed and accurate records of the learning experiences of each student are available and revisions can be made on the basis of actual student responses. By revising the programme on the basis of the records, programmes can be developed which teach more efficiently. Thus the record left by the student in a programme serves as a powerful tool for learning about learning.

Programmed Learning implies auto instruction. A genuine programmed learning material can be distinguished from other types of learning materials on the following attributes :

(i) Guaranteed Comprehensibility

Besides promoting effective learning, programmed learning ensure full understanding of the subject matter.

(ii) Tested efficiency

Before being conducted on the intended group of learners, the programme's efficiency is tested on a small group. After the conduction of the programme, the intended learners are tested to see the efficiency of the programme.

(iii) Skip-Proof Feature

The programme is so designed that the learner has to go through each and every frame in order to attain the terminal goal.

(iv) Self Correcting Feature

The learner is immediately confirmed if he has answered correctly. If he is wrong, he gets corrected by checking his response with the correct response supplied by the programmer.

(v) Automatic encouragement

As the correct response is reinforced, the learner gets automatic encouragement.

(vi) Diagnostic Feature

Remedial instruction can be provided as the programme helps the teacher to diagnose the learner's difficulties.

4. Styles of Programming

Within last two decades, various styles of programming have emerged. There is a wide flexibility shown in the choice of styles used for making programmes. Programmed material can be presented to the learner either in book form or through teaching machine or a computer in the following popular styles:

1. Linear or Extrinsic model of programming
2. Branching or Intrinsic model of programming
3. Mathetics and
4. Computer Assisted Instruction (C.A.I.)

Linear style of programming was developed and popularized by B.F. Skinner. He developed this style on the basis of his theory of 'Operant conditioning'. The operant conditioning principles and methods that appear to work so successfully in training animals are assumed to «apply to human learning as well.

A linear programme is also called extrinsic programme as the instructional sequence is extrinsically controlled by the programmer. The mechanism of the iinear programme is that the learner; is presented with information through logically structured small steps known as frames, and called upon to answer a question. As soon as he responds he is shown the correct answer to confirm his response. This confirmation serves the same reinforcing function for humans as a food pellet serves for a rat. If a student responds incorrectly to a particular frame, he may have to repeat the frame or he may be told what the correct response is.

The second basic form of programming is intrinsic programming or Branching. This type of programming was first invented by Pressey for the use with his original teaching machine in 1926. In 1950, this method was developed further by Crowder. This style of programming is called intrinsic because herein the learner within himself adapts the instruction to his needs. In Crowder's own words branching or intrinsic programme is one which adapts to the needs of the students without the medium of any extrinsic device such as a computer. The underlying principle of branching is that different students needs different instructional materials and that students can learn from their own errors. The rationale of intrinsic programming postulates that the basic learning takes place during the student's exposure to new material. Crowder believes that learning is communication. He favours large chunks of material at a time which may convey a total concept to the learner. Crowder's technique of communication is quite different from Skinner's who believes in breaking the subject matter into stimulus-response chains. In branching the student's choice determines directly and automatically what material he will see next. The learner controls the exact sequence that he will follow among available branches in the programme.

Origin

Crowder was a technician working with the United States Air Force. He had occasion to deal with vocational training of aircraft maintenance trainees who were taught to repair faults in aircraft engines. The problem before Crowder was to train the technicians to find to cause of an engine breakdown as soon as possible without first dismantling the whole engine. A good mechanic is expected to minimise the number of possible errors and this he cannot do until he puts his finger on the right one.

Practically, there is no difference in linear and branching styles as regards the preparatory stage of the programme. The second stage of writing a programme is quite different in branching style. In branching programme the information is not broken into small steps but instead is presented in large steps. The mode of response is different in branching programme. The student has to select correct response out of four or five choices. The student is routed through the branches according to his response. The paradigm appears like the following figure :-

MAIN STEAM

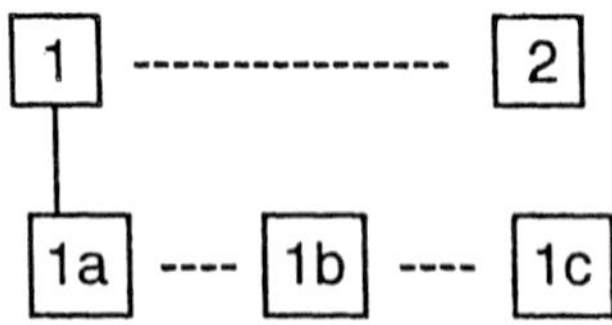

The procedure of writing frame sequence in developing a branching programme is different from that in the linear programme. There are two types of branches : main steam and remedial frames. First the programmer writes the main sequence of frames with multiple choice answers, after which he tries it on a small group of target population and decides which parts of the programme are likely to cause the greater amount of difficulty and require remedial sequences.

Thus, in contrast to linear programme which is designed to produce only correct responses, the branching programme is set up to make intelligent use of errors by leading the learner to see for himself where he went wrong. The material in a frame here is larger and much information is presented at each step. A step may consist of two or three paragraphs or even a full page. The material when presented in a book form takes the name of "scrambled book" because the pages do not follow the normal sequence. The Branching programme has serious limitations. There is every possibility that the learner may guess the correct answer without understanding the subject matter of the frame. The cost of preparing the programme is very high. This model can not be used on very small children. Infinite branching is not feasible, so we cannot cater to the needs of all individuals. Above all, the cost of preparation is very high as the programme needs frequent revisions.

Mathetics Style

The Mathetics style of programming was developed by Thomas F. Gilbert (1962). This programme is very suitable for developing programmes pertaining to the acquisition of skills. Mathetics is defined as a systematic application of the reinforcement theory to the analysis and construction of complex repertoires which represent the mastery of subject matter. The unit for mathetical sequence is called an exercise in order to distinguish it from the usual frame in programmed instruction. Retrogressive chaining represents the aspect of the mathetics approach that differentiates it from the other programming techniques.

In the Mathetics style of programming, the mastery step is taught first. In teaching a chain using this method the programmer supplies the student with all of the steps leading upto the mastery step and prompts him to perform the mastery step. Then, the programmer supplies all of the steps upto the step that immediately precedes the mastery steps, i.e. that last sub-mastery step, prompts this step and releases the students, to practice the mastery steps. Next the programmer provides all the steps, leading up to the step immediately preceding the last sub mastery and mastery steps. This is the basic concept of "Retrogressive Chaining" - demonstrate, prompt and release. The programmer continues in this manner, each time allowing the student to perform one additional step until he has worked his way back to the first step in the procedure and can perform the entire task.

The rationale for the "retrogressive chaining technique" is that the closer the student is to the reinforcement when he is being taught, the more effective the reinforcement becomes. The reinforcement in this case is the completion of the task. So the mathetical programmes utilize the principle of motivation in task completion.

The serious limitation of this programme is that starting with the end behaviour sometimes overwhelms the learners, especially the slow learners, who might otherwise, turn out excellent performers. Secondly only concrete material and subject matter involving psychomotor skills can be gainfully programmed by means of mathetic model.

Computer Assisted Instruction

Computer assisted instruction is a natural outgrowth of the application of programmed learning. The aim of programming is to provide individualized instruction to meet the special needs of each learner. The computer can store organized information and use selected portion to meet the needs of individual learners. Programmers develop programmes and fit them into particular computers. Computer is not a type of programming, it is rather a device used to bring home the instructional material to the learners.

Adjunctive Programming

Some programmers do not prefer to adhere to a particular style. They are of the opinion that any style which seems to be appropriate for a particular material may be selected by the programmer for a specific population. Psychologists like Pressey are of the opinion that a usual text book should be combined with some programmed material so that learning takes place more effectively. Thus combining the basic technique, of programming with writing of an ordinary text book is another style of programming. Such a technique is called adjunctive programming.

Pressey and others who believe that self-instruction should be an adjunct to teaching rather than the main medium, take a very different view of programming from those who prefer to remain Skinnerians or Crowderians or Gilbertians. According to Pressey's (1963) point of view, the initial presentation of most types of instructional material should not be bits and pieces but in larger, meaningful whole. Most often this would be by text book, but it might be by field trip, demonstration, or experiment. After the first presentation has given the learner a chance to 'move about freely in the material' and to grasp its larger structure, self instruction might well be used to enhance the clarity and stability of the subject matter.

PART B

1. Rationale of the Study

Programmed Learning is the first application of the experimental studies with the help of laboratory conditions to be used in the learning process. The principles of programmed learning materials which have been enumerated, in Part A of this chapter, are such that they make the student master the subject while making very few errors. Remedial instruction can be provided as the programme helps the teacher to diagnose the learner's difficulties.

In India, there is a dearth of programmed learning materials. All the teaching is done by the conventional methods of teaching and provides no motivation to the students. Programmed Learning stimulates both students and teachers. Sometimes the teacher may fail to clarify the subject matter through the text book and lectures. Here programmed learning is an effective instructional device.

The researcher, has chosen Home-Science as the subject for the development of the programmes because of its importance in practical life. The girls of today will be mothers of tomorrow. They will be able to comprehend the subject matter properly, when they are given instructions through programmed learning materials.

Since programmed learning material ensures near percent mastery of the subject matter, the programmes in Home Science will certainly motivate intended group of learners to attain cent percent mastery of content and further enable them to apply this knowledge in real life like situations. The researcher herself has studied Home Science as one of the major subjects during her graduate studies. These factors motivated the researcher to select the topic of research. A few researchers have ventured to evolve and validate programmed learning materials in India. A very few researchers have ventured to develop programmes in the subject of Home Science.

Parlikar (1979) made a study on the suitability of programmed learning in Home Science Education for adolescent girls. The findings of the study revealed that programmed leaning materials were suitable for promoting Home Science education. Jeyachandran (1980) made an experimental study of the efficacy of programmed film strips as a method of teaching history. The result revealed that retention of learning was more in case of programmed film strips in comparison with conventional method of teaching.

Pandey (1980) made a study on the use of programmed instruction in teaching mathematics. He found out that the group following programmed text was significantly superior in retention to the group following the traditional method.

Sheshadri (1980) developed programmed learning materials of branching type in mathematics. He found them to be more effective than the conventional method of teaching.

Inamdar (1981) studied the effectiveness of programmed learning in the subject of mathematics. The results, conveyed that the programmed learning technique was superior to conventional technique.

Mavi (1981) developed and empirically validated programmed learning materials in physical geography. He found the opinion of the students towards the programme as favourable.

Shah (1981) developed and validated programmed learning materials in mathematics. He found the reaction of students and teachers favourable towards the programme.

Sharma (1981) developed a programme and a criterion test on classification of plant kingdom.

Suthan (1981) developed programmed learning material in algebra. He found that the programmed learning material was superior to the traditional way of teaching.

Rabindradas (1984) found that Self Instructional Material (SIM) on health education developed by him for students resulted in better learning than the conventional classroom teaching. Learners also expressed a more positive attitude towards SIM.

In a somewhat similar study, Sangnan (1984) reported better performance of B.Ed., students who learnt through PLM developed in linear style when compared to the achievement of the students who were taught in the usual classroom. On testing the effectiveness of PLM prepared for secondary students in geography, Chaudhri (1985) found that after perusing PLM students gained significantly as far as knowledge of the subject has concerned. The material was equally effective for both rural and urban students.

By and large the findings are in favour of programmed learning material.

2. Objectives of the Study

The following were the objectives of the study selected by the researcher :

(i) Development of programmed learning materials in Home Science.

(ii) Empirical validation of programmed learning materials.

3. Hypothesis

"Ninety percent of the learners are able to perform on the ninety percent of the frames correctly.".

4. Statement of the Study

"Development And Empirical Validation of Programmed Learning Material In Home Science on Food And Nutrition for Twelfth Grade Students."

5. Procedure

For developing and validating programmes on the proposed unit, the programmes went through the following four-phases :

STAGE I : Preparatory Analysis

STAGE II : Development of the Programmes

STAGE III : Try out for modification

STAGE IV : Evaluation of the programmes

STAGE I : Preparatory Analysis

During the preparation stage, the following steps were covered by the researcher :

1.1 Selection of the topics.

1.2 Writing assumptions about the learners.

1.3 Content analysis of the selected topics.

1.4 Writing instructional objectives in behavioural terms.

1.5 Writing prerequisite knowledge and skills in behavioural terms.

1.6 Developing the criterion tests on the selected topics.

1.7 Evolving-the core material.

The researcher has discussed the above mentioned steps in more details in Chapter 2.

Stage II : Development of the Programmes

While writing programmes on the selected topics, the researcher took the following decisions:

2.1 Decision about the medium and style of the programmes for each topic. The medium of each programme was English. The style of the programmes is Hybrid.

2.2 Frames were developed in consonance with the selected programming style. Appropriate care was taken to make use of priming, prompting, fading and testing techniques.

2.3 The researcher made final adjustments of sequences. After having tried the programmes on the target student populations, some alterations were made by the researcher.

2.4 Editing

The draft programmes evolved by the researcher were got edited by the following experts in the following hierarchy:

2.4.1 Editing by subject matter expert.

2.4.2 Editing by programming technique expert. This included:

(a) Editing the individual frames.

(b) Editing the composite programme.

2.4.3 Editing by the language expert.

Stage III : Try out for modification

The duly edited programmes evolved by the researcher were tried out unit wise as follows :

Individual Try Out

The programme was administered in an informal situation to five students on a single learner at a time. The purpose of individual try out was to disclose as many programme inadequacies as possible. The inadequacies were eliminated and the time taken on each frame was noted.

Small group Try Out

After making the changes based on individual try out, the programme was presented to a small but representative group of ten learners for whom the programme was written. This helped the researcher in adequately revising the frame content and the sequence of the frames.

Final Field Try Out

This was the final trial of the programme. The entire programme in its final form was administered to the total group of students. A group of 100 students were taken intentionally, to see the effect of the programme in its finished form.

Stage IV : Evaluation of the programmes

On the basis of the data collected in the final try out, the programmes were evaluated unit wise in terms of :

1. Error Rate
2. Programme Density
3. Criterion Test
4. Gain Ratio
5. Sequence Progression
6. Attitude Co-efficient.

Chapter 2

PREPARATORY ANALYSIS

The preparatory analysis of the programme included the preparation of the programmes. The steps included in the preparatory analysis are listed below :

1) Selection of the topics to be programmed.
2) Writing assumptions about the learners.
3) Preparation of content outline i.e. content analysis.
4) Defining objectives on behavioural term.
5) Defining prerequisite knowledge and skills in behavioural terms.
6) Constructing test items for assessing terminal behaviour i.e. preparing criterion tests.
7) Writing the core material.

In this chapter, a detailed analysis of every step listed above has been made. The researcher followed this procedure while developing the programmed learning materials.

STEP I

SELECTION OF THE TOPICS TO BE PROGRAMMED

The researcher, selected a part of the syllabus prescribed by the Punjab School Education Board for XIIth grade students of Home Science. All the topics of the course from the part of "Foods and Nutrition" were selected for programming. The whole subject of Home Science for Twelfth grade students was not programmed, because the part on child and mother's craft can easily be taught by the conventional method of teaching.

The researcher applied the criteria suggested by Espich and William in their book "Developing Programmed Instructional Materials" for developing the programmes. These criteria are given below. The researcher has tried to explain how she developed the programmes, keeping the criteria in mind.

I. Should the Topics be Programmed

The researcher, first decided the feasibility of the topics in terms of their utility. In selecting the topics, a number of questions helped her. These questions are enumerated below:

1.1 **Is the subject matter stable** ? The researcher selected topics having stable subject matter. Although, after new findings and researches new things keep adding to the topics of Food and Nutrition the subject matter does not undergo frequent changes.

1.2 The second consideration which was kept in mind before developing the programmes was that ***Is the programme already available***? In India, a very few programmes have been developed in Home Science. So far, no programme has been developed for twelfth grade students on Foods and Nutrition in Punjab.

1.3 Another question which was kept in mind before developing of the programmes was that ***is the time available to complete the programmes***. Since, the writing of the programmes is a time consuming task, the researcher limited her study on Food and Nutrition and prepared programmes for XIIth class.

1.4 The fourth question which the researcher kept in mind before developing the programmes was that will the *programme help in solving teaching learning problems ?* The researcher did not select the topics which can be conveniently taught by other methods.

II. The second criteria suggested by Espich and William is that ***Are the objectives of the teaching training realistic ?***

The researcher saw to it that the objectives of the learning material are real and useful for XIIth grade students of Home Science. The objectives of each programme have been defined in behavioural terms in the later part of this chapter.

III. The third criteria was that will the results justify the expense ?

The researcher saw to it that the expenses on developing the programmes were justifiable in terms of gains obtainable from the programmes. The programmes will be useful for XIIth grade students, who have opted Home Science.

IV. The fourth criteria suggested by Espich and Williams is that ***Can the desired results be measured ?***

The researcher has stated her objectives of content in behavioural terms. She was able to design criterion test of each programme keeping these in mind. Thus the terminal performance of the learner can be measured after the finishing of each programme.

V. The fifth criteria, kept in mind while developing the programme was that ***does the topic curtail to the instructor's burden?***

All the programmes that have been developed, curtail the teacher's burden. Since all the topics that have been programmed are a part of the syllabus of Home Science for twelfth grade students they are going to relieve the burden of the instructor.

The entire course of Foods and Nutrition was selected by the researcher keeping in mind the above criteria. The different units to be programmed have already been listed in the second part of this chapter. The contents of these units have a logical structure and include facts and structured information.

The researcher has chosen Foods and Nutrition as the subject for the development of the programmes because of its importance in practical life. The girls of today will be mothers of tomorrow. They will be able to comprehend the subject matter properly, when they are given instructions through programmed learning. Since programmed learning material ensures near cent percent mastery of subject matter, the programmes in Home Science will certainly motivate intended group of learners to attain cent per cent mastery of content and further enable them to apply this knowledge in real life situations.

The subject on Food and Nutrition has been dealt within a scientific manner. The researcher divided the content to be programmed broadly into two sections viz. Food and Nutrition. The section on food was further subdivided into seven parts. The researcher developed programmes for all the six nutrients in the section on Nutrition. The subsection on vitamins was further subdivided into Fat - soluble vitamins and water soluble vitamins.

The topics rendered in the programmed form are as follows :

PART A : FOOD

A - 1 Concept of Food and Nutrition

A - 2 Functions of Food

A - 3 The Digestion of Food

A - 4 Advantages of Cooking

A - 5 Methods of Cooking

A - 6 Causes of Food Spoilage

A - 7 Principles of Food Preservation

PART B : NUTRITION

While preparing the programmes on nutrients, the researcher dealt with the following aspects of each nutrient separately :

(a) Composition

(b) Function

(c) Requirements

(d) Effects of Deficiency

(e) Food Sources

The researcher developed the programmes for the following nutrients :

B - 1 Proteins

B - 2 Carbohydrates

B - 3 Fats

B - 4 Water

MINERALS

B - 5 Calcium

B - 6 Phosphorus

B - 7 Sodium

B - 8 Potassium

B - 9 Iron

B - 10 Iodine

VITAMINS

FAT SOLUBLE VITAMINS

B - 11 Vitamin A

B - 12 Vitamin D

B - 13 Vitamin E

B - 14 Vitamin K

WATER SOLUBLE VITAMINS

B - 15 Vitamin C

B - 16 Vitamin B_1 (thiamine)

B - 17 Vitamin B_2 (Riboflavin)

B - 18 Vitamin B_3 (Niacin)

B - 19 Vitamin B_6 (Pyridoxine)

B - 20 Vitamin B_{12} (Cyanocobalamin)

B - 21 Pantothenic Acid

B - 22 Folic Acid

B - 23 Biotin

B - 24 Choline

B - 25 Inosital

STEP II

WRITING ASSUMPTIONS ABOUT THE LEARNER

After selection of the topics on the basis of the criteria suggested by Espich and William, the researcher wrote down the assumptions about the learners, for whom the programmes were to be prepared. It is essential to have a brief reference of the age, skills, socio-cultural background, intellectual level and general scholastic abilities of the learner.

The assumptions about the learners for whom the programmes were made are given below :

1) ***Age*** : 16+
2) ***Class*** : XII
3) ***Gender*** : Females
4) ***Skills*** : The learners can read and write English.

   They can comprehend the material and have manipulative skills.
5) ***Interests*** : The learners have keen interest in Home Science.
6) ***Socio-cultural Background***: The learners come from diverse socio-economic strata. They generally hail from urban area.
7) ***Intellectual level*** : Average and above average.
8) ***Scholastic Abilities*** : Generally first and second divisioners. The researcher gathered the above information from the learners, their teachers and the cumulative records maintained in the office.

STEP III

PREPARATION OF CONTENT OUTLINE

The third step involved in the preparation of the programme was content outline. This includes the major instructional content in terms of major course concepts. The researcher chose the concept keeping two things in mind. Firstly, she kept in view the basic assumptions about the learners. Secondly, she kept in view the course of study prescribed for 12th grade students of Home Science by the Panjab School Education Board.

The researcher could have elaborated her study enormously since a lot of research has been done of Food and Nutrition and there is ample knowledge available on these topics. However, she delineated the study and developed the programmes keeping in view the intellectual capacity of the twelfth grade students. The researcher has limited herself to the syllabus prescribed for twelfth grade students.

The programmes which the researcher has constructed are listed unit - wise below :

PART A : FOOD

Unit No. A. 1 Concept of Food and Nutrition

Unit No. A. 2 Functions of Food

2.1 Physiological functions of food.

2.2 Psychological functions of food.

2.3 Social functions of food.

Unit No. A 3 The Digestion of food

3.1 Mechanical and chemical phase of Digestion.

3.2 Digestion of food in the mouth.

3.3 Digestion of food in the stomach.

3.4 Digestion of food in the small intestine.

3.5 Digestion of food in the large intestine.

Unit No. A 4 Advantages of cooking

Unit No. A 5 Methods of Cooking

5.1 Cooking by the application of water.

5.2 Cooking with steam.

5.3 Cooking by fats and oils.

5.4 Cooking by hot dry air.

5.5 Microwave cooking.

Unit No. A 6 Causes of Food Spoilage

6.1 Spoilage due to micro-organisms.

6.2 Spoilage due to enzymes.

6.3 Spoilage due to environmental factors.

Unit A - 7 Principles of Food Preservation

7.1 To safeguard against micro-organisms.

7.2 To safeguard against enzymes.

7.3 To safeguard against environmental factors.

PART B: NUTRITION

B - 1 Proteins

1.1 Composition of Proteins.

1.2 Functions of Proteins.

1.3 Requirement of Proteins.

1.4 Food sources of proteins.

1.5 Effects of Deficiency of Proteins.

B-2 Carbohydrates

2.1 Composition of carbohydrates.

2.2 Functions of carbohydrates.

2.3 Requirement of carbohydrates.

2.4 Food sources of carbohydrates.

2.5 Effects of Deficiency of Carbohydrates.

B-3 Fats

3.1 Composition of fats.

3.2 Functions of fats.

3.3 Requirement of fats.

3.4 Effect of Deficiency of fats.

3.5 Food sources of fats.

B-4 Water

4.1 Composition of water.

4.2 Functions of water.

4.3 Requirement of water.

4.4 Effect of deficiency of water.

4.5 Sources of water.

MINERALS

B-5 CALCIUM : Its composition, function, requirement, food sources and effects of deficiency.

B-6 PHOSPHORUS : Its composition, function, requirement, food sources and effects of deficiency.

B-7 SODIUM : Its composition, functions, requirement, food sources and effects of deficiency.

B-8 POTASSIUM : Its composition, function, requirement, food sources and effects of deficiency.

B-9 IRON : Its composition, function, requirement, food sources and effects of deficiency.

B-10 IODINE : Its composition, function, requirement, food sources and effects of deficiency.

VITAMINS

FAT SOLUBLE VITAMINS

B-11 Vitamin A : Its composition, function, requirement, food sources and effect of deficiency.

B-12 Vitamin D : Its composition, function, requirement, food sources and effect of deficiency.

B-13 Vitamin E : Its composition, function, requirement, food sources and effect of deficiency.

B-14 Vitamin K : Its composition, function, requirement, food sources and effect of deficiency.

WATER SOLUBLE VITAMINS

B-15 Vitamin C : Its composition, function, requirement, food sources and effect of deficiency.

B-16 Vitamin B_1 : Its composition, function, requirement, food sources and effect of deficiency.

B-17 Vitamin B_2 : Its composition, function, requirement, food sources and effect of deficiency.

B-18 Vitamin B_3 : Its composition, function, requirement, food sources and effect of deficiency.

B-19 Vitamin B_6 : Its composition, function, requirement, food sources and effect of deficiency.

B-20 Vitamin B_{12} : Its composition, function, requirement, food sources and effect of deficiency.

B-21 Pantothenic Acid : Its composition, function, requirement, food sources and effect of deficiency.

B-22 Folic Acid : Its composition, function, requirement, food sources and effect of deficiency.

B-23 Biotin : Its composition, function, requirement, food sources and effect of deficiency.

B-24 Choline : Its composition, function, requirement, food sources and effect of deficiency.

B-25 Inosital : Its composition, function, requirement, food sources and effect of deficiency.

STEP IV

SPECIFICATION OF OBJECTIVES IN BEHAVIOURAL TERMS

The specification of objectives in behavioural terms is considered as a very important step in the preparatory analysis. Behavioural objectives are always stated in specific terms in order to attain specific learning outcomes. A behavioural objective indicates what the student should be able to do after she finishes the programme. Thus, the specification of objectives in behavioural terms, helped the researcher to evaluate the effect of the quality of the programmes on the learners.

The researcher followed the three objectives suggested by Robert Mager, in his book "Preparing Instructional Objectives" while writing the behavioural objectives of her programme. Mager suggests that a programmer should write objectives by asking three questions :

1) What will the student be doing when he is demonstrating proficiency ?
2) Under what condition will this behaviour occur?
3) What is the level of acceptable performance ?

The first question refers to the behaviour of the learner which can be observed. For example 'Mentions the seven advantages of Cooking' .... 'Names two major animal sources of Vitamin A', 'Mentions, the three principles of cooking'.

The second question suggested by Mager refers to the conditions under which the leaning will take place. An example of this is given below :

When shown a diagram of the human digestive system the learner is able to locate the small intestine and label its three sections.

The third question refers to the standard of acceptable performance. For example, the student mentions any seven advantages of food.

The content and completeness of objectives is a very important task in the preparatory analysis. The researcher constructed a complete list of objectives which specified the knowledge that a student must possess in order to demonstrate the mastery. A complete list of objectives helped in breaking down major objectives into component skills and knowledge and thus helped in indicating exactly what the student must learn if she has progressed from the level of entering behaviour to terminal performance.

Keeping in mind Mager's three questions for writing the objectives, the researcher wrote the objectives of thirty two selected topics in behavioural terms which are written unit wise below. Every objective stated in behavioural terms is the performance which is accepted from the student after she has finished the programme.

After reading the programmes the student performs the following tasks with reasonable accuracy.

UNIT A : FOOD

A-1 CONCEPT OF FOOD AND NUTRITION

1.1 Defines the term 'NUTRITION' in her own words.

1.2 Classifies Nutrients according to their chemical composition by naming the 6 major classes of nutrients.

1.3 Classifies the nutrients according to their four functions.

1.4 Differentiates between the terms 'Malnutrition', 'under-nutrition' and 'over-nutrition'.

1.5 Classifies and lists the four basis of division of food as per their function.

1.6 Specifies the sources of the four division of food as per their function.

1.7 Classifies and lists the four basis of division of food as per their nutrients.

A-2 FUNCTIONS OF FOOD

2.1 Gives the three foundations of food under the following three broad headings namely physiological functions, psychological functions and social functions.

2.2 Analyses the three broad functions of food and further classifies them into eight functions.

2.3 Names the most abundant body building material in the body and lists the six body building nutrients got from food.

2.4 Names the nutrient which does not play a role in the regulation of body processes.

2.5 Enlists the three factors on which the energy requirements of an individual depend.

A-3 THE DIGESTION OF FOOD

3.1.1 The learner when presented with a diagram of the human digestive system names all its parts correctly.

3.1.2 The learner defines in a few lines the process of digestion.

3.1.3 Explains the physical phase of digestion.

3.1.4 Explains the chemical phase of digestion

3.1.5 Explains in her own words the progress of food through the mouth.

3.1.6 The learner names the enzyme secreted in the mouth that helps in the digestion of food.

3.1.7 Writes the role played by pharynx and oesophagus in the digestion of food.

3.2 The student on her own explains the progress of food through the stomach, by writing the changes which the food undergoes in the upper and lower parts of the stomach.

3.2.1 Names the four substances of gastric juice.

3.2.1 Enlists the function of each substance of gastric juice.

3.3 Given the diagram of the human digestive system, the student locates the small intestine and labels its three sections.

3.3.1 Explains the progress and digestion of food through the small intestine.

3.3.2 Mentions the functions of villi, bile and the pancreas in the digestion of food.

3.3.3. Without any external aid the student explains the process by which carbohydrates are converted into glucose, fructose and galactose in the small intestine.

3.4 When shown an unlabelled diagram of the digestive system, the student locates the large intestine.

3.4.1 Writes the names of the four regions of the large intestine.

3.4.2 The student explains the progress and digestion of food in the large intestine.

A-4 ADVANTAGES OF COOKING

4.1 Enlists seven advantages of cooking

4.2 Cites at least two examples each to show how cooking makes food tasty and how cooking adds variety in the daily diet.

4.3 Names the changes brought about by cooking food

4.4 Explains how cooking helps in making the digestion of food easy.

A-5 METHODS OF COOKING FOOD

5.1 Enlists the five major methods of cooking food.

5.2 Explains how cooking is done by the application of water, giving the three methods of cooking done with the application of water.

5.3 Enlists atleast two advantages and two disadvantages of boiling, stewing and simmering giving atleast two examples of foods that are cooked by the above mentioned processes.

5.4 Mentions the two methods of cooking food by steam.

5.5 Writes at least two lines each to describe the process of direct steaming, indirect steaming and pressure cooking.

5.6 Enlists atleast two advantages, and two disadvantages of steaming and pressure cooking.

5.7 Names the three types of frying and explains in atleast two lines the difference among the three.

5.8 Mentions atleast two advantages and two disadvantages of frying foods.

5.9 Enlists atleast four advantages of cooking food by hot dry air and atleast two disadvantages of baking.

5.10 Mentions the three ways by which cooking is done by hot dry air.

5.11 Mentions atleast one advantage and one disadvantage of microwave cooking.

A-6 CAUSES OF FOOD SPOILAGE

6.1 Names the three major causes of food spoilage.

6.2 Enlists the conditions under which micro-organisms, yeast and mould can grow.

6.3 Writes two lines each on bacteria, yeast and mould. She should be able to mention the conditions which bacteria, yeast and mould need to thrive.

6.4 Writes the meaning of Hyphae.

6.5 Enlists the methods by which enzyrne activity can be prevented.

6.6 Enlists the factors in the environment which cause food spoilage

6.7 Names the rodents which cause food spoilage

6.8 Explains in atleast two lines how food is spoiled by light and moisture.

A-7 PRINCIPLES OF FOOD PRESERVATION

7.1 Enlists the principles of food preservation and its methods.

7.2 Explains in atleast two lines how food can be preserved by refrigeration.

7.3 Explains in atleast four lines the method of preserving food by dehydrofreezing.

7.4 Differentiates between dehydrofreezing and freeze drying.

7.5 Explains how food is preserved by the method of dehydration citing examples of dehydrated foods.

7.6 Explains in atleast two lines the role of heat in the process of canning.

7.7 Names, the oldest and the newest forms of food preservation.

7.8 Writes in two lines the effect which radiation has on the pathogenic bacteria present in the food.

UNIT-B : NUTRITION

B-1 PROTEINS

1.1 Composition of Proteins

1.1.1 Specifies the elements of which proteins are composed.

1.1.2 Mentions the number of amino acids present in proteins.

1.1.3 Classifies proteins on the basis of their amino acid make up.

1.3.4 Classifies proteins according to their nutritive value.

1.2 Functions of Proteins

1.2.1 Enlists the various functions of proteins.

1.2.2 Specifies the amount of energy provided by 1 gm of protein.

1.2.3 Specifies the function of proteins in adults and in children.

1.3 Requirement of Proteins

1.3.1 Specifies the daily requirement of proteins in adult man.

1.3.2 Specifies the daily requirement of proteins in pregnant woman.

1.3.3 Specifies the daily requirement of proteins in children.

1.3.4 Specifies the daily requirement of proteins in adolescents.

1.3.5 Specifies the daily requirement of proteins in infants.

1.4 Food sources of Proteins

1.4.1 Enlists the rich food sources of proteins.

1.4.2 Mentions the animal sources rich in proteins.

1.4.3 Enlists the poor sources of proteins.

1.5 Effect of deficiency of Proteins

1.5.1 Names three diseases which occur due to deficiency of proteins.

1.5.2 Enlists the constant, symptoms of Kwashiokar.

1.5.3 Enlists the constant symptoms of Maramus.

B-2 CARBOHYDRATES

2.1 Composition of carbohydrates

2.1.1 Specifies the composition of carbohydrates by naming the elements of which carbohydrates are composed.

2.1.2 Mentions the three categories into which carbohydrates can be divided.

2.1.3 Enlists the characteristics of mono-saccharides.

2.1.4 Enlists the characteristics of disaccharides.

2.1.5 Enlists the characteristics of Polysaccharides.

2.1.6 Distinguishes between mono-saccharides, disaccharides and polysaccharides.

2.2 Functions of Carbohydrates

2.2.1 Enlists the various functions of carbohydrates.

2.2.2 Mentions the amount of energy provided by Carbohydrates.

2.2.3 Explains, in two lines how carbohydrates help to maintain water and sodium levels.

2.3 Requirement of carbohydrates

2.3.1 Names the cheapest food source of energy in the diet.

2.3.2 Mentions the factors on which the carbohydrate availability in the diet will depend.

2.3.3 Mentions the amount of carbohydrate that must be present in the daily diet.

2.4 Food Sources of Carbohydrates.

2.4.1 Names the major plant sources which provide carbohydrates.

2.4.2 Mentions in percentage the amount of sugar got from fresh fruits.

2.4.3 Names the four different plant sources of carbohydrates.

2.4.4 Names the animal sources of carbohydrates.

2.5 Effect of Deficiency of Carbohydrates

2.5.1 Names the condition which results from a carbohydrate deficient diet.

2.5.2 Explains in two sentences, the complications arising due to ketosis.

2.5.3 Enlists the conditions arising due to deficiency of carbohydrates.

B-3 FATS

3.1 Composition of Fats

3.1.1 Names the elements of which fats are composed.

3.1.2 Defines oils in one sentence.

3.1.3 Names the main constituents of lipids.

3.1.4 Distinguishes between simple lipids, compound lipids and derived lipids.

3.2 Functions of Fats

3.2.1 Enlists the seven functions of fats.

3.2.2 Specifies the amount of energy provided by 1 gm fat.

3.2.3 Names the tissue in which the excess of fat is stored.

3.2.4 Names the vitamins which fats carry.

3.2.5 Explains in one sentence how the subcutaneous layer of fat helps the body in cold weather.

3.2.6 Explains how fats act as protein sparer.

3.3 Requirement of Fats

3.3.1 Mentions the requirement of fats required for the human body.

3.4 Food Sources of fats

3.4.1 Names the richest source of fats in the diet.

3.4.2 Names atleast two animal sources of fats.

3.4.3 Names atleast two plant sources of fats.

3.5 Effect of Deficiency of Fats.

3.5.1 Enlists the conditions which are caused by the deficiency of fats.

3.5.2 Names the disease caused by the deficiency of fats in infants.

3.5.3 Mentions the effect of deficiency of fats on fat soluble vitamins.

B-4 WATER

4.1 Composition of Water

4.1.1 Specifies the percentage of water in the total body weight.

4.1.2 Differentiates between intracellular and extracellular water.

4.1.3 Mentions the principal cation in the cell wall.

4.1.4 Names the principal cation in the extracellular fluid.

4.1.5 Writes in percentage the water contents of different parts of the body.

4.1.6 Explains the percentage of water variation in the body.

4.2 Functions of Water

4.2.1 Enlists the six functions of water.

4.2.2 Explains in two sentences the function of water as a carrier or nutrients and waste.

4.2.3 Lists the parts of the body which water lubricates.

4.2.4 Elucidates the role of water as a regulator of water temperature.

4.2.5 Explains in two sentences the role of water in the regulation of body temperature.

4.3 Requirement of water

4.3.1 Names the safe guide for the requirement of water.

4.3.2 Specifies the requirements of water for a normal individual.

4.3.3 Differentiates the water requirements of an infant and adult.

4.3.4 Enlists the factors on which the water requirements of the body depend.

4.3.5 Specifies the conditions under which the water requirement is more.

4.4 Sources of water

4.4.1 Mentions the ways in which water is lost from the body.

4.4.2 Specifies the amount of water intake and water lost in the body.

4.4.3 Enlists the sources of water in the body.

4.4.4 Mentions the foods which are good sources of water.

4.4.5 Mentions the foods which are poor sources of water.

4.5 Effects of Deficiency

4.5.1 Mentions the three effects of deficiency of water in the body.

4.5.2 Enlists the evidence of dehydration in the body.

4.5.3 Explains the effect of dehydration on the skin.

4.5.4 Mentions the ways in which excess water is lost through the body.

4.5.5 Explains the effect on the functioning of the kidneys as a result of deficiency of water.

4.5.6 Explains the effect on the utilization of nutrients as a result of deficiency of water.

MINERALS

B-5 CALCIUM

5.1 Composition of calcium

5.1.1 Specifies the percentage of calcium present in bones and teeth.

5.1.2 Specifies the percentage of calcium present in blood and tissues.

5.2 Functions of Calcium

5.2.1 Enlists the major functions of calcium.

5.2.2 Names the vitamin which calcium helps in absorbing.

5.3 Requirements of Calcium

5.3.1 Explains in two sentences, why calcium is a necessity during infancy.

5.3.2 Mentions the daily requirement of calcium for infants.

5.3.3 Mentions the daily requirement of calcium for adolescents.

5.3.4 Mentions the daily requirement of calcium for pregnant woman.

5.4 Food Sources of Calcium

5.4.1 Names four excellent food sources of calcium.

5.4.2 Names three good sources of calcium.

5.4.3 Names four fair sources of calcium.

5.4.4 Names two poor sources of calcium.

5.5 Effects of Deficiency

5.5.1 Mentions the two reasons due to which deficiency of calcium occurs in the body.

5.5.2 Names the disease caused by the deficiency of calcium in children.

5.5.3 Names the disease caused by the deficiency of calcium in adults.

5.5.4 Mentions the main symptoms of the disease Rickets.

5.5.5 Mentions the main symptoms of the disease Osteomalacia.

B-6 PHOSPHORUS

6.1 Composition of Phosphorus

6.1.1 Mentions the percentage of phosphorus present in bones and teeth.

6.1.2 Mentions the amount of .phosphorus present in 100ml blood.

6.2 Functions of Phosphorus

6.2.1 Enlists the various functions of phosphorus.

6.3 Requirement of Phosphorus

6.3.1 Specifies the amount of phosphorus required by infants in the first six months.

6.3.2 Specifies the amount of phosphorus required by infants from 6 month onwards.

6.4 Food Sources of Phosphorus

6.4.1 Names four excellent food sources of phosphorus

6.4.2 Names four good sources of phosphorus.

6.4.3 Names two poor sources of phosphorus.

6.5 Effect of Deficiency.

6.5.1 Enlists the effects which deficiency of phosphorus may cause.

B-7 SODIUM

7.1 Composition of sodium

7.1.1 Specifies the amount of sodium present in the body.

7.1.2 Specifies the amount of sodium present in the extracellular fluid.

7.1.3 Mentions the percentage of sodium ions present in the blood.

7.2 Functions of Sodium

7.2.1 Enlists four functions of sodium.

7.3 Requirement of sodium

7.3.1 Mentions in one sentence the reason for which no dietary allowances are set up for sodium.

7.3.2 Mentions the sodium requirement for an average adult.

7.3.3 Mentions the sodium requirement for people who do heavy work.

7.4 Food sources of sodium

7.4.1 Names the chief source of sodium in the diet.

7.4.2 Names the animal sources of sodium.

7.4.3 Names the commercial preparations in which sodium is found.

7.4.4 Names the poor sources of sodium.

7.5 Effects of Deficiency

7.5.1 Name the conditions in which sodium deficiency may occur.

7.5.2 Mentions the class of workers in which sodium deficiency is likely to occur.

B-8 POTASSIUM

8.1 Composition of potassium

8.1.1 Mentions of total potassium content in the human body.

8.1.2 Mentions the percentage of potassium in intracellular fluids.

8.1.3 Specifies the amount of potassium present in digestive juices.

8.2 Functions of Potassium

8.2.1 Mentions four functions of potassium.

8.2.2 Mentions in one sentence the function of potassium within the cells of the body.

8.2.3 Mentions the role which potassium plays with phosphate in the body.

8.3 Requirement of potassium

8.3.1 Mentions the average requirement of potassium in adults.

8.4 Food Sources

8.4.1 Names four animal sources of potassium.

8.4.2 Names four plant sources of potassium.

8.5 Effects of Deficiency

8.5.1 Enlists four conditions in which potassium deficiency occurs.

8.5.2 Mentions four symptoms arising out of potassium deficiency.

8.5.3 Explains in one sentence how potassium deficiency effects the heart.

B - 9 IRON

9.1 Composition of Iron

9.1.1 Mentions the amount of iron present in the blood.

9.1.2 Mentions the amount of iron present in the body.

9.1.3 Names the chief constituent of red blood cells.

9.1.4 Names the parts of the body where iron is present.

9.2 Functions of Iron

9.2.1 Enlists the major functions of iron.

9.2.2 States the importance of haemoglobin in the body.

9.3 Requirements of Iron

9.3.1 Names four conditions on which the requirement of iron in the body depends.

9.3.2 Mentions the iron requirement for infants.

9.3.3 Mentions the iron requirement for children.

9.3.4 Mentions the iron requirements for teenage girls.

9.3.5 Mentions the iron requirements for pregnant women.

9.4 Sources of Iron

9.4.1 Names three excellent animal sources of iron.

9.4.2 Names three excellent plant sources of iron.

9.4.3 Names three rich sources of iron.

9.5 Effect of Deficiency

9.5.1 Enlists the three reasons due to which deficiency of iron occurs.

9.5.2 Names the condition which occurs due to deficiency of iron.

9.5.3 Enlists the causes due to which Anemia occurs.

9.5.4 Enlists the symptoms of Anemia in children.

B-10 IODINE

10.1 Composition of Iodine

10.1.1 Mentions the quantity of iodine present in the body.

10.1.2 Mentions the quantity of iodine present in the thyroid gland.

10.2 Functions of Iodine

10.2.1 Enlists four functions of iodine.

10.2.2 Enlists the three functions of thyroxin.

10.2.3 Names the vitamin, in the conversion of which iodine helps.

10.3 Requirements of Iodine

10.3.1 Mentions the daily iodine requirement for infants.

10.3.2 Mentions the daily iodine requirement for adults.

10.4 Food Sources of Iodine

10.4.1 Names the most important source of iodine.

10.4.2 Names the sea-foods which are rich in iodine.

10.4.3 States, the fact on which the iodine content of vegetables depends.

10.5 Effects of Deficiencv

10.5.1 Enlists four effects which deficiency of iodine causes.

10.5.2 Names the condition caused by enlargement of thyroid gland.

10.5.3 States the symptoms of Myxodema.

10.5.4 States the symptoms of Cretinism.

VITAMINS

B-11 VITAMIN A

11.1 Composition of Vitamin A

11.1.1 Names the various forms of Vit. A.

11.1.2 Mentions the effect of heat and light on Vit. A.

11.1.3 Mentions the colour of Vit. A.

11.2 Functions of Vitamin A

11.2.1 Enlists the various functions of Vitamin A.

11.2.2 Mentions in one line the role of Vit. A in proper vision.

11.2.3 Mentions in one line the role of Vit. A in maintaining the epithelial tissues.

11.3 Requirement of Vitamin A

11.3.1 Mentions the Vit. A requirement for men.

11.3.2 Specifies the Vit. A requirement for women.

11.3.3 Enlists the Vit. A requirement for adults.

11.3.4 Specifies the Vit. A requirement for Children.

11.4 Sources of Vit. A

11.4.1 Enlists the animal sources of Vit. A.

11.4.2 Names the plant sources of Vit. A.

11.4.3 Mentions the richest source of Vit. A.

11.4.4 Explains in two sentences the effect of cooking on Vit. A.

11.5 Effects of deficiency

11.5.1 Enlists the effects of deficiency of Vit. A in the body.

11.5.2 Mentions the symptoms of night blindness.

11.5.3 Mentions in one sentence the role of Vit. A in tooth formation.

11.5.4 Mentions the symptoms of Xerothalmia.

B-12 VITAMIN D

12.1 Composition of Vitamin D

12.1.1 Mentions the effect of heat on vitamin D.

12.1.2 Mentions the name of the organic compound to which Vit. D belongs.

12.2 Functions of Vitamin D

12.2.1 Enlists the five functions of Vit. D.

12.2.2 Explains in five lines the role of Vit. D in proper utilization of calcium and phosphorus.

12.2.3 Explains in a sentence the role of Vit. D in regular heart beat.

12.3 Requirements of Vitamin D

12.3.1 Mentions the three reasons for which it is not possible to measure the requirements of Vit. D.

12.3.2 Mentions three conditions in which the requirement of Vit. D increases.

12.4 Sources of Vit. D

12.4.1 Names the major source of Vit. D.

12.4.2 Names the major food sources of Vitamin D.

12.5 Effects or deficiency

12.5.1 Enlists the five effects of deficiency of Vitamin D.

12.5.2 Mentions the main symptoms of Rickets.

12.5.3 Enlists the main symptoms of Osteomalacia.

12.5.4 Enlists the main symptoms of the disease 'Tetany'.

B-13 Vitamin E

13.1 Composition of Vitamin E

13.1.1 Mentions the colour of Vit. E.

13.1.2 Mentions in two lines the effect of heat on Vitamin E.

13.1.3 Mentions the effect of ultraviolet rays on Vit. E.

13.2 Functions of Vitamin E

13.2.1 Enlists the five functions of Vitamin E.

13.2.2 Explains the role of Vit. E as an antioxidant in one sentence.

13.3 Requirement of Vit. E

13.3.1 Mentions the Vit. E requirement for infants.

13.3.2 Mentions the Vit. E requirement for children.

13.3.3 Mentions the Vit. E requirement for adults.

13.3.4 Mentions the Vit. E requirement for pregnant women.

13.4 Sources of Vit. E

13.4.1 Writes the names of vegetables rich in Vit. E

13.4.2 Writes the names of the whole grains rich in Vit. E

13.4.3 Writes the names of oils rich in Vit. E.

13.4.4 Writes the names of good sources of Vit. E.

13.4.5 Writes the names of bad sources of Vit. E.

13.5 Effect of Deficiency

13.5.1 Mentions the reason for the low possibility of Vit. E deficiency.

13.5.2 Names the 3 deficiencies of Vitamin E.

B-14 VITAMIN K

14.1 Composition

14.1.1 Names the two forms of Vit. K.

14.1.2 Name colour of Vit. K.

14.1.3 Mentions the effect of heat on Vit. K.

14.1.4 Mentions the effect of cooking on Vit. K.

14.2 Functions of Vitamin K

14.2.1 Enlists the functions of Vitamin K.

14.2.2 Elucidates in two sentences the role of Vit. K in blood coagulation.

14.3 Requirements of Vit. K

14.3.1 Enlists the conditions when the need of increase in Vit. K. is required.

14.3.2 Mentions the Vit. K requirements for new born infant.

14.3.3 Mentions the Vit. K requirement for the mother at the time of labour.

14.4 Sources of Vit. K

14.4.1 Enlists the green leafy vegetables rich in Vit. K.

14.4.2 Names the animal sources of Vitamin K.

14.4.3 Names the poor sources of Vit. K.

14.5 Effects of Deficiency

14.5.1 Mentions the reasons for which there is poor absorption of vitamin K.

14.5.2 Mentions the effects of deficiency of vitamin K.

WATER SOLUBLE VITAMINS

B-15 VITAMIN C

15.1 Composition

15.1.1 Mentions the colour of Vit. C.

15.1.2 Names the 3 elements of which Vit. C is composed.

15.1.3 States the effect of acidic medium on Vitamin C.

15.1.4 States the effect of alkaline medium on Vitamin C.

15.2 Functions of Vit. C

15.2.1 Enlists the functions of Vitamin C.

15.2.2 Names the mineral, the absorption of which, is enhanced with Vitamin C.

15.2.3 Explains in one sentence the role of Vit. C in the healing of wounds and burns.

15.2.4 Explains in one sentence how vit. C acts as an infection fighter.

15.2.5 Explains in one sentence the role of Vit. C in preventing colds and frost bites.

15.3 Requirements of Vit. C

15.3.1 Mentions the requirements of Vit. C for infants.

15.3.2 Mentions the requirements of Vit. C for adults.

15.3.3 Mentions the requirements of Vit. C for pregnant women.

15.4 Food Sources

15.4.1 Names the main food sources of Vit. C.

15.4.2 Enlists the points to be followed in order to get maximum content of Vit. C from available food stuffs.

15.5 Effects of Deficiency.

15.5.1 Names the diseases caused by the deficiency of Vit. C.

15.5.2 Mentions the reasons due to which deficiency of Vitamin C occurs.

15.5.3 Names the symptoms of scurvy.

15.5.4 Explains in one sentence how Vit. C deficiency causes anemia.

15.5.5 Elucidates the importance of Vit. C for arthritis patients.

THE B VITAMINS

B-16 VITAMIN B_1 (THIAMINE)

16.1 Composition.

16.1.1 Names the scientist who isolated thiamine from rice and bran.

16.1.2 States the colour of thiamine.

16.1.3 Mentions the taste of thiamine.

16.2 Functions of Thiamine.

16.2.1 Enlists the functions of thiamine.

16.2.2 Explains in two sentences the role thiamine plays in the functioning of the heart.

16.2.3 Explains in two sentences, how thiamine helps in meeting the needs of the nerves.

16.2.4 Mentions the function of thiamine as a catalyst.

16.2.5 Elucidates in two lines, how thiamine is necessary for growth.

16.2.6 Explains in two lines how thiamine is necessary for the proper functioning of red blood cells.

16.3 Requirements of Thiamine

16.3.1 Mentions the thiamine requirement for children.

16.3.2 Mentions the thiamine requirement for adults.

16.3.3 Mentions the thiamine requirement for pregnant women.

16.4 Sources of Thiamine

16.4.1 Names the cereals rich in thiamine.

16.4.2 Names the pulses rich in thiamine.

16.4.3 Names the nuts and seeds rich in thiamine.

16.4.4 Mentions the names of food stuffs rich in thiamine.

16.5 Effects of Deficiency

16.5.1 Enlists the complications arising out of lack of thiamine.

16.5.2 Enlists the main symptoms of dry beri-beri.

16.5.3 Enlists the main symptoms of wet beri-beri.

B-17 VITAMIN B_2 (RIBOFLAVIN)

17.1 Composition

17.1.1 Mentions the structure of Vit. B_2.

17.1.2 Mentions the effect of heat on Vit. B_2.

17.1.3 Mentions the taste of Vit. B_2.

17.1.4 States the effect of light on Vit B_2.

17.2 Functions of Vit. B_2

17.2.1 Enlists the functions of Vit. B_2.

17.2.2 Explains in two lines the role of Vit. B_2 in protein metabolism.

17.3 Requirement of Vit. B_2

17.3.1 Mentions the requirement of Vit. B_2 for adults.

17.3.2 Mentions the requirement of Vit. B_2 for children.

17.3.3 Mentions the requirement of Vit. B_2 for infants.

17.3.4 Mentions the requirement of Vit. B_2 for lactating women.

17.4 Sources of Vit. B_2.

17.4.1 Names the meat products rich in Vit. B_2.

17.4.2 Names the pulses rich in Vit. B_2.

17.4.3 Names the milk products rich in Vit. B_2.

17.4.4 Names the poor sources of Vit. B_2.

17.5 Effects of Deficiency.

17.5.1 Explains in two lines how Vit. B_2 deficiency causes photophobia.

17.5.2 Mentions the effects of deficiency of Vit. B_2 on the skin.

17.5.3 Mentions the effect of deficiency of Vit. B_2 on the liver.

B-18 VITAMIN B_3 (NIACIN)

18.1 Composition.

18.1.1 Names the two forms of Vit. B_3.

18.1.2 Explains in one sentence why Vit. B3 is a unique B Vitamin

18.2 Functions of Vit. B_3

18.2.1 Enlists the functions of Vit. B_3.

18.2.2 Explains in two lines the role of Vit. B_3.

18.3 Requirement

18.3.1 Mentions the Vit. B_3 requirement for adults

18.3.2 Mentions the Vit. B_3 requirement for children

18.3.3 Mentions the Vit. B_3 requirement for infants

18.3.4 Mentions the Vit. B_3 requirement for pregnant women.

18.4 Food Sources

18.4.1 Names the cereals which are good sources of Vit. B_3.

18.4.2 Names the richest source of Vit. B_3.

18.4.3 Names the food stuffs rich in Vit. B_3.

18.5 Effects of Deficiency

18.5.1 Names the disease caused by the deficiency of Vit. B_3.

18.5.2 Mentions the main symptoms of Dermatitis.

18.5.3 Mentions the main symptoms of Diarrhoea.

18.5.4 Mentions the main symptoms of Dementia.

B-19 VITAMIN B_6 (PYRIDOXINE)

19.1 Composition

19.1.1 Names the scientist who discovered Vit. B_6.

19.1.2 Names the three forms of Vit. B_6.

19.1.3 Mentions the effect of heat on Vit. B_6.

19.2 Functions of Vit. B_6

19.2.1 Enlists the four functions of Vit. B_6.

19.2.2 Explains in two sentences the role of Vit. B_6 in activating enzymes.

19.2.3 Explains the role of Vit. B_6 in protein metabolism

19.3 Requirement of Vit. B_6

19.3.1 Mentions the Vit. B_6 requirement for infants

19.3.2 Mentions the Vit. B_6 requirement for children

19.3.3 Mentions the Vit. B_6 requirement for adults

19.3.4 Mentions the Vit. B_6 requirement for pregnant women.

19.4 Food Sources of Vit.B_6

19.4.1 Names the principal sources of Vit.B_6.

19.4.2 Names the foods containing fair amount of Vit.B_6

19.5 Effects of Deficiency

19.5.1 Mentions the effect of deficiency of Vit.B6 on adults.

19.5.2 Mentions the effect of deficiency of Vit.B6 on children.

B-20 VITAMIN B_{12} (CYANOCOBALAMIN)

20.1 Composition

20.1.1 Explains in a sentence why Vit. B_{12} is the most complex of all vitamins.

20.1.2 Names the colour of Vit.B_{12} in promoting maturation of Red Blood Cells in two sentences.

20.2 Functions of B_{12}

20.2.1 Enlists the functions of Vit. B_{12}.

20.2.2 Explains in two sentences how Vit. B_{12} prevents tobacco blindness.

20.3 Requirement of Vit.B_{12}

20.3.1 Mentions Vit. B_{12} requirement for infants.

20.3.2 Mentions Vit. B_{12} requirement for children.

20.3.3 Mentions Vit. B_{12} requirement for adolescents.

20.3.4 Mentions Vit. B_{12} requirement for adults.

20.3.5 Mentions Vit. B_{12} requirement for pregnant women

20.4 Sources of Vit. B_{12}

20.4.1 Names the animal sources of Vit. B_{12}.

2.0.4.2 Names the richest source of Vit. B_{12}.

20.5 Effect of Deficiency.

20.5.1 Mentions the main symptoms of anemia.

B-21 PANTOTHENIC - ACID

21.1 Names the scientist who discovered pantothenic acid.

21.2 Mentions the taste of pantothenic acid.

21.3 Enlists two functions of pantothenic acid.

21.4 Mentions the requirements of pantothenic acid for adults.

21.5 Mentions the requirements of pantothenic acid for children.

21.6 Mentions the requirements of pantothenic acid for pregnant women.

21.7 Names the main food sources of pantothenic acid.

21.8 Names the conditions which are caused by the deficiency of pantothenic acid.

B-22 FOLIC ACID

22.1 Names the colour of folic acid.

22.2 Explains in two sentences how folic acid got its name.

22.3 Mentions the effect of heat on folic acid.

22.4 Enlists four functions of folic acid.

22.5 Mentions the folic acid requirements for infants.

22.6 Mentions the folic acid requirements for children.

22.7 Mentions the folic acid requirements for adults.

22.8 Mentions the folic acid requirements for pregnant women.

22.9 Names the richest source of folic acid.

22.10 Names the poorest source of folic acid.

22.11 Names the disease caused by the deficiency of folic acid.

22.12 Names the main symptoms of anemia.

B-23 BIOTIN

23.1 Names the colour of Biotin.

23.2 Mentions the effect of acids on Biotin.

23.3 Mentions the two functions of Biotin.

23.4 Mentions the requirement of Biotin for infants.

23.5 Mentions the requirement of Biotin for children.

23.6 Mentions the requirement of Biotin for adults.

23.7 Mentions the requirement of Biotin for pregnant women.

23.8 Names rich sources of Biotin.

23.9 Names moderate sources of Biotin.

23.10 Names poor sources of Biotin.

23.11 Mentions the effect of deficiency of Biotin.

B-24 CHOLINE

24.1 Mentions the colour of choline.

24.2 Mentions the effect of acids on choline.

24.3 Mentions the effect of alkalis on choline.

24.4 Enlists three functions of choline.

24.5 Mentions excellent sources of choline.

24.6 Mentions good sources of choline.

24.7 Mentions fair sources of choline.

24.8 Mentions the, effect which deficiency of choline can cause.

B-25 INOSITAL

25.1 Mentions the taste of Inosital.

25.2 States the effect of heat on Inosital.

25.3 Mentions the function of Inosital.

25.4 Names the sources of Inosital.

The specification of a terminal behaviour is effective only when there is a starting line drawn. Thus the formulating of the behavioural objectives was a very essential step in order to make the learning through the programmes effective.

STEP V

WRITING PRE-REQUISITE KNOWLEDGE AND SKILLS IN BEHAVIOURAL TERMS

Before going through the programme the learner

1. Reads effectively the text books of Home - Science written in English.
2. Discusses learning difficulties encountered in the classroom.

3. Applies the theoretical knowledge of Home - Science in real life.
4. Comprehends diagrams, and other sketches *of* the digestive system and the various aspects of nutrition.
5. Comprehends tables given in different programmes.
6. Describes the importance of nutrition.

The learners, for whom these programmes have been prepared possessed these prerequisites knowledge and skills.

These prerequisites knowledge and skills assumed on the part of the learner were assessed before she was presented with the self-instructional material. These assumptions also helped the researcher in defining the objectives in behavioural terms.

STEP VI

WRITING THE UNIT TESTS

Developing of the unit tests was one of the most important steps in the preparation stage of the programme. The unit or the criterion test is designed to measure the effectiveness of some instructional objectives which are reached by an individual learner after having gone through the programme. The reason of making the unit test in the preparation stage, is to ensure that it exactly coincides with programme objectives. It's construction at this stage helped to sharpen and clarify the objectives in the researcher's mind. While setting the terminal test the researcher kept in mind the following points :

1. Questions were couched in behavioural terms, so that the answers were either right or wrong.
2. The test items are capable of interpretation in only one way and there are no ambiguities in the test item.

3. The test items were in keeping with the objectives of the programme and the conditions under which the learner worked.
4. All concepts that were taught were tested.
5. There were no prompts in unit test.

Unit tests were developed in order to check the competency attained by the learner at the end of completing the programmed material. These tests were administered to the students in the individual and small group try out sessions and were revised accordingly. Initially all the tests included test items of multiple choice and completion type of test items. Later on the researcher realised that for certain topics, all the concepts could not be tested. So, she included short type questions in the test items also. The questions which were included in the unit tests have specific answers, generally not more than two lines. For a few topics the researcher included true and false questions also.

While developing the unit test, the researcher kept in mind the reliability and validity of the test. The reliability of a criterion test has been described as the proportion of identical judgment between two judges. The validity of a criterion test implies that the test truly measures what it purports to measure. The validity of a criterion test is estimated in three ways :

1. ***Descriptive Validity***: It depends upon the accuracy of the test's descriptive capabilities. Here the learner's performance can be accurately interpreted according to the domain description.
2. ***Functional validity***: It implies the accuracy with which a criterion test satisfies the purpose to which it is being put.
3. ***Domain selection validity*** : It implies the accuracy with which the domain selection was made.

All the above mentioned estimates of validity of a criterion test are not made by statistical formulae, but are based on simple judgmental analysis made by subject matter experts. The researcher got the unit tests checked from subject experts in Home Science.

STEP VII

WRITING THE CORE MATERIAL

Writing the core material was the last step in the preparation of the programme. This was a very important step because only if there was a suitable content structure, could the programme be made. The researcher wrote down the complete information and the list of all diagrams that would be included in the programme. She kept in mind the objectives, while she was writing the core material. She wrote the core material in a straight prose narration.

While writing the core material the researcher consulted the text book prescribed for XIIth class students of Home Science. Besides this she consulted various other books on Foods and Nutrition. In order to keep her information updated she consulted several journals. The core material was written in simple language and was cross checked by consultation of subject dictionaries, encyclopedias and source books on the selected topics. Subject experts were also consulted for ascertaining the validity of the chosen content.

The mechanism of actual writing of the programmes has been described in the next chapter.

Chapter 3

DEVELOPMENT OF THE PROGRAMMED UNITS

After completing the preparatory stage of the programmed material systematically, the researcher was able to start the writing of the actual programmes. At this stage the researcher prepared the core material of different units of the course on Home Science. The content outline, behavioural objectives and criterion test based on the assumptions about the learner which had already been prepared by the researcher provided sufficient background for the preparation of the core material.

The first unit of the programme namely "Concept of Food and Nutrition" was programmed first. It was tried out on a group of 5 students, on a single student at a time. After modifying it, the programme was again tried out on a small group of 8-9 students. On the basis of this try out the programme was further modified. Then it was got cyclostyled for field try out. The other programmed units were developed on the basis of the experiences of the programme on the unit of the Concept of Food and Nutrition.

While developing the programmes, the researcher followed the linear style of programming. The frames generally were of constructed response type. There were only a few frames which required the students to select the response out of the alternative responses given. The use of such frames was made very sparingly so that the students did not guess the responses. Table 3.1 shows in detail the number and nature of the frames contained in each programme. In all the frames the student were asked to make on overt response. These overt responses provided the data on the basis of which the programmes were revised.

TABLE 3.1

Unit No.	*Unit Title*	*Total No. of Frames*	*Constructed Response*	*Selection Response Types Frames*
A :	FOOD			
A-1	Concept of Food and Nutrition	51	51	0
A-2	Functions of Food	50	50	0
A-3	The Digestion of Food	156	153	3
A-4	Advantages of Cooking	34	34	0
A-5	Methods of Cooking	106	105	1
A-6	Causes of Food spoilage	55	54	1
A-7	Principles of Food Preservation	45	44	1
B :	NUTRITION			
B-1	Proteins	71	66	5
B-2	Carbohydrates	93	90	3
B-3	Fats	44	44	0
B-4	Water	45	45	0
MINERALS				
B-5	Calcium	42	41	1
B-6	Phosphorus	35	35	0
B-7	Sodium	40	40	0

Unit No.	*Unit Title*	*Total No. of Frames*	*Contructed Response*	*Selection Response Types Frames*
B-8	Potassium	36	36	0
B-9	Iron	52	50	0
B-10	Iodine	50	50	0
VITAMINS				
B-11	Vitamin A	53	52	1
B-12	Vitamins D	52	46	6
B-13	Vitamin E	30	30	0
B-14	Vitamin K	23	23	0
B-15	Vitamin C	36	36	0
B-16	Vitamin B_1 (Thiamine)	35	35	0
B-17	Vitamin B_2 (Riboflavin)	30	30	0
B-18	Vitamin B_3 (Niacin)	34	34	0
B-19	Vitamin B_6 (Pyridoxine)	24	24	0
B-20	Vitamin B_{12}	27	27	0
B-21	Pantothenic Acid	16	16	0
B-22	Folic Acid	25	25	0
B-23	Biotin	20	20	0
B-24	Choline	16	16	0
B-25	Inosital	15	15	0
Total		1441	1419	22

The frame sequences developed by the researcher follow the matrix approach of programming. In a few frames, the ruleg and ergrul approach of sequencing have been followed. However, in the major part of the frames the matrix approach of sequencing has been followed. The concepts have been taken in order of their increasing difficulty and the frame sequences have been developed accordingly.

PRESENTING THE MATERIAL IN FRAMES AND DECIDING ON INFORMATION ELEMENTS

A frame is a small segment of the subject matter which is presented to the student at a time. Each frame calls forth a particular response from the learner. While presenting the material in frames, the researcher followed the guidelines suggested by Markle, in her book, "Good Frames and Bad A Grammar of Frame Writing."

In each frame the researcher tried to provide those stimuli, which were considered necessary to evoke the student's response. The frames were designed according to the increasing difficulty of concepts. The introductory frames given at the start of each programme were full of prompts, so that the chances of making mistakes by the learner were reduced. After the introductory frames, the teaching frames were given. These frames were followed by practice frames. Practice frames were put so that the learner was able to grasp the material she was learning. At the end of each programme, the testing frames were put. These did not impart any new knowledge to the learner but were a sort of revision for the learners.

The researcher inserted panels in some of the programmed sequences. The panels were included to impart additional information to the students. In some programmes panels were inserted to show diagrams and tables to the learners. The frames which followed each panel were based upon the study of that panel. The learners could respond to these frames only when they studied these panels carefully.

Each frame contains a sub-unit of the subject matter. The frames have been so constructed, that they call forth a particular response from the students. While designing the frames the researcher provided prompts, so as to make it easier for the learners to learn and to produce a reliable response from them. In the introductory frames the stimuli are the words which follow the blank in the next frame.

Each frame in the programme provides a very small piece of information to the student. Only a little material is provided to the learner at one time so that the chances of making errors decrease. Sometimes, frames comprising of many sentences have been inserted in the programme. These frame are large, since they impart only a single concept to the learner. The researcher, however, has tried her best to ensure that each frame does not consist of more than three to four sentences.

NATURE OF RESPONSE REQUESTS

The response which the learner is asked to make is a very important feature of the programme. The responses which the learners were asked to make were always dependent upon some important part of the subject matter. The frames which were based on panels had responses, which the learner could make only if she had read the subject matter properly. Mostly the frames had constructed response type answers. Only a few frames had selection response type answers. These frames were such which the researcher felt would be difficult for the learner to answer without giving a strong prompt. The researcher tried to keep the blanks, where the learner had to put the responses at the end of each frame. This was done, in order to ensure that the learner read the whole frame.

Another, important aspect of the nature of the response requests, was that the learners were asked to make overt responses only. The researcher decided that the frames would have overt responses only, because covert responses are not amenable to observation. Moreover, overt responses were required for trying out the programmes. Therefore, the selection of overt responding was done so that a proper record of the responses made by the learners was available to the researchers in a written form. This record helped the researcher later, in calculating error rates, detecting faulty frames for modification and drawing flow charts for inspection of sequence progression.

Richard Anderson (1967) points to two conclusions which considerable empirical support to overt responding.

1. Overt responding, facilities learning when responses are relevant to the content of the lesson and
2. Overt responding should be required in the learning of unfamiliar and technical terms.

Both these conditions are inherent in the self-learning material developed by the researcher.

All the responses, which the learners were asked to make were related to the content that had been taught to them through the frames or through the panels. The students were asked to write down their answers on the programme itself. Ample space had been provided for the learners to write down their responses. Each student was asked to mention her name, section and roll number at the beginning of the programme.

Asking for overt responding was in fact a practical necessity for the researcher. It was on the basis of the complete written record that the researcher was able to make revisions in the programme . The written record also helped the researcher in determining the learning behaviour of the students. A major difficulty which some of the students faced was that they could not understand the meanings of some words which were given in the frames. The majority of these students were those who had taken Hindi or Punjabi as their medium of instruction.

The researcher did not consider it necessary to make the programmes in Punjabi and Hindi, because the standard of English she used in the programmes was not very difficult. Also all of the students who have taken Home Science are required to answer a compulsory subject of English. So, all of the students have a working knowledge of English.

The wrong responses which the students made were, sometimes due to their negligence. Sometimes, the meaning of the words were nor clear to them because the words were not a part of their working vocabulary. A number of mistakes were made by the students in the topic on 'The Digestion of Food'. The main reason for this was that the chapter was difficult for them as all the students are arts students. The researcher inserted a number of panels in the chapter to make it easier for the learners. Although most of the students, were able to respond 75% of the frames correctly, they were not able to comprehend the whole content contained in the topic.

Sometimes, the students made wrong responses, due to their eagerness to finish the programme quickly. The researcher did not include these students in the final results she prepared.

During the individual and small group try out situations, it was on the basis of the response requests that the researcher was able to amend the programme. In some response requests the students could not answer because they could not understand the meaning of the frames correctly. The researcher changed the language of such frames in the final field try out.

DECISION ON RESULT INDICATION

One of the major characteristics of programmed learning materials is that of making a provision for the correct response with which the student can compare her own response. When the student discovers her response to be correct, she obtains confirmation; when the response is incorrect, she receives correction. A good programmer should elicit a series of responses from the learner.

Researchers, differ in their views regarding the nature of response request. Some researchers like Krumboltz and Weisman (1962) found no difference in the test performances of students who were supplied the correct answers all the time and of those who were supplied the correct answer only part of the time. They suggest that supplying the correct response may be more important later than earlier in the programme, when most of the prompts for the correct responses are withdrawn.

The researcher provided the correct response with each frame. In most of the frames, the blank space technique of response was used. The missing word or words were supplied by the student in the blank space provided in the programme itself. In a few frames, binary choice was given and the student had to choose the correct answer.

The confirmatory responses were provided at the bottom of each page. The researcher tried to vary the format locations of the confirmatory responses during individual and small group try out situations. During the individual tryout the confirmatory responses were written on the back page of the frame, whereas during small group try out the confirmatory responses were provided at the bottom of each page. The researcher found that the changing of format locations did not effect student's interaction with the programmed material. They learnt equally from these different sets of arrangements. The researcher decided to give the confirmation responses at the bottom of the each page so that the students would not have any difficulty in confirming the results.

USE OF PROMPTS TO GUIDE STUDENT'S RESPONSE

A prompt or cue is an additional stimulus which increases the probability of a correct response. The researcher has made use of various types of prompts in the programmes to make it easier for the students to comprehend the material. According to Markle (1964) Prompts are supplementary stimuli in that these are added to a frame to make the frame easier but are not sufficient in themselves to produce the response. The researcher made use of prompts for the following two purposes :

1. Prompts guide the learner to correct response without over controlling his behaviour.
2. Prompts prevent the student from making unnecessary errors.

The researcher used the prompts in introductory and teaching frames only. In the practice frames prompts were gradually withdrawn and no prompts were used at all in the criterion frames.

The researcher made use of various prompting techniques while providing the prompts in the frames. She made the maximum use of temporal (or sequence) prompts and panels. In a few frames the copy prompts were also used. The researcher did not make use of this type of prompting often, because in this type of prompting no understanding of the subject matter is required from the students. This type of prompting was used by the researcher when the students were required to learn something difficult. For example in the chapter on Vitamins, the students were made familiar with the requirements of each vitamin through this type of prompt.

Another prompting technique used by the researcher was the temporal or sequence prompt. In this technique the information required to make the correct response was contained in the preceding frame. The main advantage of the temporal prompt was that the learner had to concentrate in order to respond as he must remember information previously given. In the various programmes which the researcher made she used the panels as prompts. The panel itself is a prompt because the student first reads the information given in the panel and then with the help of the panel answers problems contained in the accompanying frames.

The maximum use of prompts was made in the teaching frames. This was done to ensure maximum probability of success. After a point had been taught, adequate opportunity for practice to reinforce the desired behaviour was given to the students. Each new point was followed by practice frames and prompts were gradually withdrawn. This development, is referred to as 'weaning' stage and the technique of gradual withdrawal of prompts is called 'vanishing' or 'fading'. At the end of each programme criterion frames were provided. The criterion frames were completely unprompted in order to adequately test content mastery of the subject content.

While writing frames proper care was taken by the researcher to arrange them in an ordered sequence. The frames were adjusted in the programme on the basis of their increasing order of difficulty. The researcher tried to use unambiguous words. The researcher tried to ensure that the language used in the programmes was easy so that all the students had a working knowledge of it. The programme was read and re-read by the researcher in order to ensure that correct information was provided to the students in an ordered sequence. The responses required by the learners were within their capabilities. The material was not too easy so that it would not result in boredom. The researcher tried to take maximum care to ensure maximum probability of success on every frame on the part of the learner.

EDITING AND REVIEW OF THE PROGRAMMED UNITS

Since, the programme is to be given to the learners, in order to teach them something new, it was very essential that all technical or other mistakes were removed from the programme. After having completed the first draft of the programmed units, these were subjected to a through editing and reviewing process. This was done to remove the inadequacies of language used in the frames, to check the logical sequence of frames, to check the diagrams and to check the material provided in the frames.

The preliminary draft of the programmes was taken to a lecturer on Home Science. The inaccuracies in the subject matter, panels and diagrams were discussed with her and modified accordingly. She advised the researcher to make the use of tables at some places so as to make the learning process easier. She also advised to researcher as to where diagrams should be put.

The second person in the hierarchy of editing is the expert in the programming technique. The researcher got her programmes edited one by one. She made the changes in the format locations of the confirmatory responses on the advise of the programming technique expert.

The third person in the hierarchy of editing was the language expert. He checked the language of the frames, spelling, grammatical mistakes and punctuation forms. The language expert is an English teacher in the University.

The suggestions made by the subject matter expert, programming technique expert, and language expert contributed sufficiently towards the improvement of programmes developed by the researcher. These persons also provided encouragement for accomplishing the task more efficiently and accurately.

Chapter 4

TRY OUT FOR MODIFICATION

This chapter deals with the try out of the programmes after the researcher completed the first draft of the programme. The programmed units were subjected to experimental try-outs three times namely :

1) Individual try out
2) Small group try out
3) Final Field testing

These three types of experimental tryouts are explained as follows :

INDIVIDUAL TRY OUT

In the individual try out, the programmes which were developed by the researcher were administered on five learners in an informal situation, one at a time on a single learner. The student, on whom the individual try out was done, represented broadly the target population on whom the field try out were later on administered. The student was given neatly hand written programme in an informal situation. The student was told that she was helping in making a successful programme. She was asked to note down the number of all the frames which she found difficult in the programme. After the programme had been finished by the student discussion of the difficulties in each programme was made with the student. Discussion was made with the student orally, because this helped in clarifying the problem areas more explicitly. Also sometimes, after working through the programme the student is unable to list all the difficulties because this demands diagnostic and verbal ability which may be beyond the student's capability. The researcher noted down all the difficulties which the student had encountered while working through the programme. Thus, individual try out helped the researcher in removing the ambiguities in the frames of the programmes. All the programmes were edited and revised unit wise on the basis of the suggestions rendered by the student in the individual try out experiments.

SMALL GROUP TRY OUT

After editing and revision on the basis of individual try out, the programmes were rewritten in a definite form. The responses were given at the bottom of each page. Although, there are many formats of locating confirmatory responses, the researcher presented the down the page format due to several reasons. The students were not familiar with the method of learning through programmes, so it was easy for them to go through the programme and confirm their response on the same page. Since, the confirmatory response was given at the bottom of each page there is little chance that the student will copy and write down the frame.

The programmes were got typed and given to a group of ten students. The researcher explained to the students as to how they should proceed through the programme. The students were asked to underline the difficult words and write "Difficult" on the frames which they could not respond. After the students had done the programme the researcher made revisions on the basis of the small group try out. The difficult words were replaced by simpler words. Some frames were further redesigned in order to make these easy for the students to respond correctly. At some places, where the students could not respond correctly on the completion type responses, selection type responses were inserted by replacing the completion type.

After the students had finished the programme they were given unit tests. On the basis of their results test items were reformulated. The results of the unit tests ensured that the programmed learning material was able to bring about the behavioural changes in terms of learning outcomes from the students.

FINAL FIELD TESTING

After the draft programme was made as satisfactory as the researcher could make it on the basis of individual and small group try out , the programmes were prepared for the field testing. All the programmes were typed neatly and then cyclostyled. Photostat copies of the diagrams were also enclosed in the body of the programmes.

The sample of the study for the final field testing were students of XII the class. All these students were girls and had opted for Home Science as one of the optional subjects. The syllabus of all the students was same i.e. syllabus prescribed by the Panjab School Education Board. The programme was tried on both school and college students. The detailed break down of the experimental sample for final field try out was :

Government Girls Senior Secondary School Mall Road Amritsar.	45
B.B.K D.A.V. College for Women Lawrance Road, Amritsar	30
Government Model Senior Secondary School Patiala	25
	Total = 100

Before administering the programmes, the researcher took permission from the Principal of the institution concerned. The concerned teachers were than contacted. The teachers extended their full co-operation. Generally the programmes were administered twice in a week.

At the beginning of each programme every student was given written instructions as to how she should proceed through the programme. Every student was given one copy of the programme. She was asked to give the response on the programme itself. She was required to write the answer in the blanks provided in each frame. Generally the students took 40 to 50 minutes to complete the programme. The programmes which were larger in size took longer time. In the case of such programmes the researcher requested the teacher in charge to give the practical periods for the working of the programme.

After the completion of the programme the student deposited the programme on which she had worked with the teacher in charge. After that she was given the unit test. She completed it and deposited it with teacher.

After the completion of the programmes, the researcher discussed the difficulties encountered by the students while working through the programmes. More difficulties were encountered by the students who had Punjabi and Hindi as their medium of instruction. Although, these students were able to work on the programmes they had some difficulty in comprehending certain technical words. Although the programmes were written in simple English, sometimes these students were unable to recall the meaning of difficult words of vocabulary. Their suggestions were invited for making the programmes more effective.

The modification in the programmes were not done tentatively. The responses made by the students were subjected to a systematic analysis. The researcher was able to make a list of faulty frames in the programmes on the basis of the field testing. Also, the field try out experiment proved to be useful for calculating error rates and for preparing the flow charts for knowing the progression of sequence. The attainment scores of the learners on the unit tests were helpful in ascertaining the gains of the programmes in terms of behavioural changes i.e. in learning outcomes.

After the completion of the tryouts of the programmes, and taking the unit tests, the students were required to go through a reaction check list. This was designed to elicit students reactions towards the developed programmes.

Chapter 5

EVALUATION OF THE PROGRAMMES

After the completion of the final field try out for modifying the programmes the researcher evaluated the programmes in terms of :

1) Error Rates
2) Programme Densities
3) Sequence Progression
4) Attainment scores on unit tests (Criterion tests) and gain ratio.
5) Students evaluation of the programmes in terms of attitude coefficient.

The proceeding discussion deals with the above mentioned terms separately :

INTERPRETATION OF ERROR RATES

Table 5.1 illustrates the error rates of the entire programmes and Table 5.2 illustrates the error rates of the subsections. All the programmes which were developed by the researcher are linear programmes. Skinner, set the criterion of such programmes to be 90-90. He desired that the errors made by the students on linear programmes should be less and that 90 percent of the students must be able to perform correctly on 90 percent of the frames in the programme.

Table 5.1 : Showing Error Rates and Cumulative Densities

Unit No.	*Unit Title*	*Error Rate in % age*	*Cumulative Density*
PART A : FOOD			
A - 1	Concept of Food and Nutrition	2.9%	0.6
A - 2	Functions of Food	3.7%	0.6
A - 3	The Digestion of Food	3%	0.6
A - 4	Advantages of Cooking	5.1%	0.6
A - 5	Methods of Cooking	2.8%	0.6
A - 6	Causes of Food Spoilage	5.6%	0.6
A - 7	Principles of Food Preservation	5.6%	0.8
PART B : NUTRITION			
B - 1	Proteins	2.4%	0.6
B - 2	Carbohydrates	2.5%	0.5
B - 3	Fats	4.8%	0.7
B - 4	Water	4.4%	0.6
B - 5	Calcium	5.07%	0.7
B - 6	Phosphorus	6.8%	0.8
B - 7	Sodium	6.9%	0.7
B - 8	Potassium	6.2%	0.7
B - 9	Iron	4.2%	0.5
B - 10	Iodine	4.5%	0.6
B - 11	Vitamin A	2.7%	0.7
B - 12	Vitamin D	3.6%	0. 6
B - 13	Vitamin E	6.1%	0.7
B - 14	Vitamin K	6.1%	0.7

Unit No.	*Unit Title*	*Error Rate in % age*	*Cumulative Density*
B - 15	Vitamin C	5.8%	0.7
B - 16	Vitamin B_1(Thiamine)	2.8%	0.8
B - 17	Vitamin B_2 (Riboflavin)	4.3%	0.8
B - 18	Vitamin B_3 (Niacin)	4.2%	0.7
B - 19	Vitamin B_6 (Pyridoxine)	4.2%	0.8
B - 20	Vitamin B_{12} (Cyanocobalamin)	3.5%	0.7
B - 21	Pantothenic Acid	4.4%	0.8
B - 22	Folic Acid	3.3%	0.8
B - 23	Biotin	4.3%	0.8
B - 24	Choline	3.7%	0. 6
B - 25	Inosital	4.3%	0.7

TABLE 5.2 : Error Rate (ER) and Independent Densities (ID) on the sub-sections of the programmed units.

UNIT No.		*I*	*II*	*III*	*IV*	*V*	*VI*	*VII*
PART A : FOOD								
A-1	ER	2.6%	3%	3%				
	ID	0.9	0.7	0.6				
A-2	ER	3.9%	5%	2.2%				
	ID	0.6%	1	0.9				
A-3	ER	1.9%	3.7%	2.5%	2.3%	2.5%	4.2%	2.1%
	ID	0.8	1	0.7	0.7	0.8	0.7	0.8
A-4	ER	5.8%	3.6%					
	ID	0.7	0.7					
A-5	ER	3.7%	2.2%	2%	2%	3.3%	3.2%	
	ID	0.6	0.9	0.8	0.9	10.9		

UNIT No.		*I*	*II*	*III*	*IV*	*V*	*VI*	*VII*
A-6	ER	7.3%	6.3%	4.1%	4.3%			
	ID	0.7	0.8	0.7	0.8			
A-7	ER	5.8%	4.8%	5.4%	8%			
	ID	0.9	0.9	0.7	0.8			
PART B	: NUTRITION							
B-1	ER	2.3%	1.9%	0.8%	2.5%	3.7%		
	ID	0.7	0.6	10.6	0.7			
B-2	ER	2.5%	1.6%	1.7%	2.7%			
	ID	0.5	0.7	0.6	0.7			
B-3	ER	5%	5.8%	3.3%				
	ID	0.7	0.8	0.8				
B-4	ER	5.9%	3.3%	3.3%				
	ID	0.8	1	0.6				
B-5	ER	5.4%	5.1%	4.7%				
	ID	0.8	0.7	0.8				
B-6	ER	4.5%	9.3%	7.8%				
	ID	0.7	1	0.8				
B-7	ER	7.7%	3.7%	8.1%				
	ID	1	0.8	0.8				
B-8	ER	6.2%	0.9	3.8%				
	ID	0.9	1	0.8				
B-9	ER	4.5%	5.8%	3.8%				
	ID	0.8	0.8	0.6				
B-10	ER	5.2%	2.7%	5.3%	4.3%			
	ID	0.8	1	0.8	0.8			
B-11	ER	3.6%	2.3%	2%				
	ID	2.6%	0.7	2%				
B-12	ER	4.9%	2.6%	3.7%				
	ID	0.7	0.7	0.7				

UNIT No.		*I*	*II*	*III*	*IV*	*V*	*VI*	*VII*
B-13	ER	8%	5.6%	4.1%				
	ID	0.8	0.6	0.7				
B-14	ER	5.1%	6.1%	7.8%				
	ID	0.8	0.9	0.6				
B-15	ER	6.1%	4.2%	6.5%				
	ID	0.8	1	0.7				
B-16	ER	2.5%	3.1%	3.2%				
	ID	0.7	0.8	0.8				
B-17	ER	4.5%	4%	4.3%				
	ID	0.8	1	0.6				
B-18	ER	3.5%	5%	5.1%				
	ID	0.7	0.7	0.8				
B-19	ER	4.6%	3.8%					
	ID	0.8	0.9					
B-20	ER	4.6%	2.6%					
	ID	0.9	0.7					
B-21	ER	4%	4.8%					
	ID	0.8	0.8					
B-22	ER	3.7%	2.8%					
	ID	0.7	0.8					
B-23	ER	5.2%	3.2%					
	ID	0.7	0.8					
B-24	ER	3%	4.3%					
	ID	0.7	0.7					
B-25	ER	4.5%	4%					
	ID	0.8	1					

Error rates were calculated on the basis of response obtainable for every frame. When a student gives an inadequate response to a frame it is considered as an error. The errors are detected by comparing the response of the student with the confirmatory response. The synonyms of certain confirmatory responses were judged as correct even though these responses did not appear in the typed programmes. Every error, made by a student on each unit was noted down, then all the errors made by all individuals on the unit were added to get a sum total of the errors made on that unit. The error rate of a unit was calculated by using the following formula :

Error Rate in percentage =

$$\frac{\text{Total No. of Errors} \times 100}{\text{Total No. of Responses} \times \text{No. of Pupils}}$$

Since, at the beginning of each unit the learner was requested to write one response per frame, the total number of responses usually equalled the total number of frames in a unit. The above formula was used to calculate the entire programmes. The error rates of each sub - section were also calculated on the same basis. The sub sections comprised approximately of more than ten frames each. In section A the subsections were made on the basis of the learning material. In section B, the learning material was divided into five broad sections i.e. composition, function, requirement, sources and effects of deficiency. In programmes with larger number of frames like in B - 1, these sections were dealt with separately. In the other units two sections, and sometimes three sections were included in a single subsection. Table III gives a detailed account of these sections.

The error rate indicates the efficacy of the programme in evoking correct responses from the learner. If the learners makes more mistakes, the error rate will be higher. Hence, lower the error rate the more efficient is the programme. As evident from Table 5.1, all the programmed units showed error rates less than 7%. Error rates of subsections (Table

5.2) did not exceed the value of 8%. The values of error rates lie within the acceptable criterion set up by Skinner. In Part B the error rates of some units exceeded 6%. This is also well within the 90 - 90 criterion set up by Skinner. 90% of the students could answer 90% the frames correctly and therefore the error rates lie within the limit acceptable for validating programmes.

If we closely examine the error rates on the sub-sections of the programme, we will find that none exceeds the percentage of 8. We can therefore safely say that 90% of the students were able to answer 90% of the frames correctly.

TABLE 5.3

Showing the frame numbers which were included in one Sub-Section, to calculate sectional error rates and independent densities.

Sub-Section of the programme showing frame numbers

Unit No.	*I*	*II*	*III*	*IV*	*V*	*VI*	*VII*	*VIII*
PART A : FOOD								
A - 1	1-13	14-38	39-51					
A - 2	1-31	32-39	40-50					
A - 3	1-27	28-36	37-50	51-66	67-95	95-144	145 to 156	
A - 4	1-22	23-34						
A - 5	1-25	26-43	44-58	59-69	70-75	76-106		
A - 6	1-23	24-29	30-46	47-55				
A - 7	1-15	16-27	28-36	37-45				
PART B : NUTRITION								
B - 1	1-22	23-37	38-46	47-52				
B - 2	1-45	46-62	63-80	81-93				
B - 3	1-14	15-31	32-44					

Unit No.	I	II	III	IV	V	VI	VII	VIII
B - 4	1-19	20-32	33-45					
B - 5	1-12	13-25	26-42					
B - 6	1-16	17-27	28-35					
B - 7	1-8	9-18	19-40					
B - 8	1-13	14-18	19-36					
B - 9	1-10	11-22	23-52					
B - 10	1-13	14-20	21-31	32-50				
B - 11	1-19	20-35	36-53					
B - 12	1-18	19-41	42-52					
B - 13	1-11	12-22	23-30					
B - 14	1-8	9-18	19-23					
B - 15	1-17	18-25	26-36					
B - 16	1-18	19-27	28-35					
B - 17	1-11	12-22	23-30					
B - 18	1-14	15-22	23-34					
B - 19	1-13	14-24						
B - 20	1-12	13-27						
B - 21	1-8	9-16						
B - 22	1-14	15-25						
B - 23	1-11	12-20						
B - 24	1-7	8-16						
B - 25	1-9	10-15						

PROGRAMME DENSITIES

The effectiveness of a programme can also be calculated by its density. The density measure of a programme reflects the difficulty level of the programme. Programme density is calculated in terms of the variety of responses expected from the learner. It is not in any way connected with the actual responses made by the learner.

The researcher used the formula 'type token ratio (TTR) prescribed by Green (1961) as a measure of density. Most of the linear programmes utilize it as an important evaluation measure. The formula used to calculate TTR is

$$\text{Density (TTR)} = \frac{Nd}{Nt}$$

Where Nd = Total number of different responses required in a programme.

Nt = Total number of responses required in a programme.

Since, in programmed learning situation, the learner is required to repeat the similar responses to various frames, the number of different types of responses is usually less than 1. The programme is easy when there is more repetition of responses.

Interpretation of Programme Densities

Cumulative Density

The density data entered in Table 5.1 reveals that in all the 32 programmes which were developed by the researcher, the cumulative density is less than one. During the small try out the density of the programmes in section B was kept lower. The researcher found that the students could work on programmes with high density. So, she rewrote the programmes, In section B all the programmes except B-2 and B-5 have density more than 0.5. In section A the densities of all the programmes is more than 0.5. Since the sample population belonged to a higher age group the, density of the programmes was purposely kept high. Also experts like Markle (1969) have proposed that during the development of the programmes, in the beginning the density of the programmes should be kept high.

Independent Densities

Table 5.2 shows the independent densities of the programmes. Here also we see that the densities are on the higher side. There are a few subsections where the density is 1. These include sub section II of unit A -2, and

A - 3, and sub - section VI of A - 5 in part A. In part B the independent densities where the density is more than one include sub section III of B - 1, subsection II of B - 4, B - 6, B - 8, B - 15, B - 17, and B - 25. In all the other sections the densities are less than 1. If we closely examine Table II we find that in all the subsections where the density is 1, the error rate is not more than 5% except in subsection II of B - 6. This goes to prove that the students were able to tolerate the difficulty level of that particular sub - section. In the small group try out when ever higher independent densities were found to coincide with high error rates, those particular sections of the programmes were modified to lower the densities. These sections were thus made easier for learning. In this manner attempt was made to reduce the error rates with the help of programme densities values, before subjecting to the final field try out.

Since the error rates are within the prescribed limit of 90 - 90 percent criterion set up by Skinner we can say that the higher density values do not create considerable problems in learning.

SEQUENCE PROGRESSION

Another measure to evaluate the effectiveness of programmed learning material is preparing flow charts of all the programmes and the criterion tests. The flow charts were prepared on graph papers.

On the horizontal side of graph frame numbers appeared, whereas on the vertical side pupil's identification numbers were given Errors made by each student on each frame were entered on these flow charts.

The identification of errors was not only important to the researcher, but it had an importance to the learners also. If the learners are informed about the mistakes they have committed on the test items immediately after the test, they can make the corrections and this will help in facilitating learning. The flow charts prepared during the initial try out were of a great help in modifying the programmes. In the final field tryout these flow charts were helpful in calculating sectional error rates.

Success on the Criterion Test

A Criterion test is a very important measure in evaluating a programmed unit. Criterion test helped to ascertain the level of performance of the students on each unit. Immediately after the student had finished working on a programme she was given the criterion test. The criterion test consisted of different test items. These included fill in the blanks, true and false items, multiple choice questions and short answer type questions had only one or two sentence answers. A unit wise analysis of the criterion tests reveals that the students made more mistakes when they were asked short answer type questions. As compared to other test items in the short answer questions, guessing of examiners is reduced. (Osterlind)

The overall percentage of success of the 100 students participating in the final field try out has been mentioned in Table 5.4. The percentage of success varied between 80% of 92%.

TABLE 5.4 : OVERALL PERCENTAGE OF SUCCESS ON UNIT TESTS

Unit No.	*Unit Title*	*Total Errors*	*Percentage of Errors*	*Success*	*Gain Ratio*
PART A : FOOD					
A - 1	Concept of Food and Nutrition	203	14.5	85.5	.85
A - 2	Functions of Food	155	12.9	87.1	.87
A - 3	The Digestion of Food	490	8.9	91	.91
A - 4	Advantages of cooking	171	10.6	89.4	.89
A - 5	Methods of cooking	218	8.0	92	.92
A - 6	Causes of Food spoilage	259	10.7	89.2	.89
A - 7	Principles of food preservation	184	10.7	9.2	

Unit No.	*Unit Title*	*Total Errors*	*Percentage of Errors*	*Success*	*Gain Ratio*
PART B : NUTRITION					
B - 1	Proteins	454	10	90	.90
B - 2	Carbohydrates	380	10	90	.90
B - 3	Fats	368	12.2	87.8	.87
B - 4	Water	314	10.8	89.2	.89
B - 5	Calcium	364	14.5	85.5	.85
B - 6	Phosphorus	272	13.6	86.4	.86
B - 7	Sodium	203	16.9	83.2	.83
B - 8	Potassium	208	17.3	82.7	.82
B - 9	Iron	207	10.3	89.6	.89
B - 10	Iodine	260	14.4	85.6	.85
B - 11	Vitamin A	242	12.1	87.9	.87
B - 12	Vitamin D	226	10.7	89.2	.89
B - 13	Vitamin E	273	15.6	84.4	.84
B - 14	Vitamin K	192	9.1	90.9	.90
B - 15	Vitamin C	266	12.6	87.4	.87
B - 16	Vitamin B_1 (Thiamine)	250	11.3	88.7	.88
B - 17	Vitamin B (Riboflavin)	220	15.7	84.3	.84
B - 18	Vitamin B_3 (Niacin)	187	15.5	84. 5	.84
B - 19	Vitamin B_6 (Pyridoxine)	208	16	84	.84
B - 20	Vitamin B_{12}	182	12.3	87.8	.87
B - 21	Pantothenic Acid	195	16.2	83.7	.83
B - 22	Folic Acid	209	16.07	83.93	.83
B - 23	Biotin	207	14.7	85. 3	. 85
B - 24	Choline	167	16.7	83.3	.83
B - 25	Inosital	138	15.3	84.7	.84

On the basis of the results on criterion tests, we can conclude that the students did learn effectively from the programmes. Better results can be obtained if the students are made to re-read the programmes.

GAIN RATIO

The gain ratio reflects the net gains obtained from learning a programmed unit. The gain ratio is calculated as the ratio difference between the actual post test score and the pre test score to the difference between the maximum possible score of post test and pre test. Thus the gain ratio takes into account the learners initial level of knowledge and skills to calculate the exact gain obtained due to experimental treatment.

The researcher used the formula given by Mcguigan and Peters (1965) to calculate the gain ratio :

Gain Ratio =

$$\frac{\text{Mean of (Post test Score - Pre test Score)}}{\text{Mean of full marks of (Post test-Pre test Score)}}$$

The percentage of mean of full marks of post test was calculated and on the basis of that, the gain ratios were calculated.

Table 5.4 gives the gain ratio obtained from the unit tests. It ranges between .80 and .90 Mcguigan and Peters (1965) suggested that the best measure of a programme's effectiveness is the gain ratio between the amount learned, and the amount that could be possibly learned. From the criterion tests and the gain ratios we can safely say that the students did learn effectively from the programmes.

ATTITUDE COEFFICIENT

The final measure of evaluating the effectiveness of a programme is the attitude coefficient. The attitude coefficient is based on an attitude scale, which was developed by the researcher and is given in the appendices. The scale, measures the attitude of the students towards the programme. It is a three point scale consisting of thirteen statements, For every statement the attitude coefficients was calculated from the responses of the learners, with the help of the formula given below :

$$\text{Attitude Coefficients} = \frac{(f^{+}) - (f^{-})}{(f^{+}) + (f^{0}) + (f^{-})}$$

Where f^{+} = Total of agreement frequencies
f^{0} = Total of neutral frequencies
f^{-} = Total of disagreement frequencies.

In Table 5.5 the attitude coefficients of 100 students participating in the tests is given.

From table 5.5 we come to know that 90% of the students found that learning through the programmes was easy. Similarly 90% of the students found the material of the programmes to be clear. 92% of the students felt that they

Table 5.5 : Showing the Attitude Coefficient

Statement Number	*Replies in Percentage (Based on the attitude scale)*			*Attitude Coefficient*
	Yes	*No*	*Uncertain*	
1.	90	7	3	0.83
2.	90	5	5	0.85
3.	92	8	0	0.84
4.	8	82	10	–0.74
5.	30	65	5	–0.35
6.	98	2	—	0.96
7.	98	2	—	0.96
8.	73	25	2	0.48
9.	98	2	—	0.96
10.	80	10	10	0.70
11.	10	78	12	0.68
12.	55	25	20	0.30
13.	0	85	15	0.85

could read the programmes easily while 8% felt that they could not read the programme easily. The above data reveals that the programmes were developed in accordance with the comprehension level of the students.

In terms of learning outcomes 98% of the students were of the view that many new things were known by reading the programmes. 80% students were of the view that they would like to study Home Science through programmes. 10% students were uncertain about whether they would like to study Home-science through programmes. This reveals that the attitude of the learners towards the programmes which the researcher has developed is quite favourable.

The students had diverse opinion on three statements. The first, statement on which they had diverse opinions was the fifth statement relating to the attention getting diverted.. Thirty percent of the students were of the view that their attention got diverted while reading the programmes, 5% students were uncertain about it and 65% students attention was not diverted. The second statement, which elicited diverse replies from the students was statement no. 8 which dealt with the student's needing the help of the teacher or a student while working through the programmes. In this case 25% of the students were of the view that they could not work on the programmes without the help of the teacher, 73% of the students could and 2% students were unsure about the statement. The students, who had to take the help of other students or the teacher were those who could not understand the meanings of certain words or could not follow some of the frames given in the programmes. The third statement which evicted a diverse response from the students was the one in which the student's opinion about the unit tests were asked. 55% of the students, were of the view that the unit tests were good, 25% were of the view that they were not and 20% were unsure about them.

The students showed a lot of interest in the programmes 98% of the students found studying Home - science through programmes interesting. 78% of the students did not find studying through programmes boring. 85% of the students were of the view that they would like to study through programmes while 15% were unsure about the statement.

The above results reveal that the attitude of the students towards the programmes was quite favourable. Most of the students were able to follow the meaning of the material that was taught through programmes. The students could learn many new things, along with finding the working through programmes interesting.

Chapter 6

CONCLUSION

INTRODUCTION

The world today is experiencing rapid technological changes. There has been an information revolution in the recent two decades. In order to make new knowledge available to the students, some innovations in the field of education are being tried out. Educational technology, which assists and supports many educational functions is a part of these innovations. Educational technology consists of hardware and software technology. The software technology refers to the detailed application by the psychology of learning to practical teaching problems. The hardware technology refers to the application of engineering principles in the development of electromechanical equipment used for instructional purposes. Programmed learning is a software technology.

RATIONALE OF THE STUDY

Programmed learning is the first systematic application of experimentally studied principles of behaviour control to the practical issues of education. It is used as a method to improve 'the teaching learning process'. It is an individualised technique of instruction, in which the student is guided to participate actively by continually making responses. Programmed learning is a process of arranging the material to be learnt in a series of small steps.

The researcher has been familiar with the subject content of Home-Science and has also learnt the technique of evolving auto-instruction programmes. Therefore for promoting the learning of Home Science students, the researcher decided to develop and empirically validate the programmed learning materials in Home-Science for Twelfth grade students.

STATEMENT OF THE STUDY

"Development And Empirical Validation Of Programmed Learning Material In Home-Science On Food And Nutrition For Twelfth Grade Students."

OBJECTIVES OF THE STUDY

(1) Development of programmed learning materials in Home-Science.

(2) Empirical Validation of programmed learning material.

HYPOTHESIS

"Ninety percent of the learners are able to perform on the ninety percent of the frames correctly."

TOOLS

(1) Programmed Learning Material

32 topics were selected from the course of Home Science for XIIth grade students of Panjab School Education Board and developed by the researcher.

The contents were programmed under two sub-sections i.e FOOD & NUTRITION

PART A : FOOD

A-1 Concept of food and nutrition.

A-2 Functions of food

A-3 The digestion of food

A-4 Advantages of cooking

A-5 Methods of cooking

A-6 Causes of food spoilage

A-7 Principles of food preservation

PART B : NUTRITION

B-1 Proteins

B-2 Carbohydrates

B-3 Fats

B-4 Water

B-5 Calcium

B-6 Phosphorus

B-7 Sodium

B-8 Potassium

B-9 Iron

B-10 Iodine

B-11 Vitamin A

B-12 Vitamin D

B-13 Vitamin E

B-14 Vitamin K

B-15 Vitamin C

B-16 Vitamin B_1 (Thiamine)

B-17 Vitamin B_2 (Riboflavin)

B-18 Vitamin B_3 (Niacin)

B-19 Vitamin B_6 (Pyridoxine)

B-20 Vitamin B_{12} (Cyanocobalamin)

B-21 Pantothenic Acid

B-22 Folic Acid

B-23 Biotin

B-24 Choline

B-25 Inosital

2) Criterion - Tests : These consist of 32 unit tests based on each unit. These were used as pretest and post test to calculate gain ratio.

3) Attitude - Scale : It is a likret type three point attitude scale developed by the researcher to measure the attitude of the students towards the programmes through which they have worked.

EXPERIMENTAL SAMPLE

The experimental sample consisted of 100 students studying Home-Science in the twelfth grade in the following institutions :

Government Girls Senior Secondary School Mall Road, Amritsar	45
B.B.K. D.A.V. College For Women Lawrance Road, Amritsar	30
Government Model Senior Secondary School Patiala	25
Total	100

PROCEDURE

The programmes were first developed by the researcher and then empirically validated. The procedure consisted of the following four stages.

STAGE I : PREPARATORY STAGE

This stage consisted of the following steps :

1.1 Selection of the topics to be programmed.

1.2 Writing assumptions about the learners.

1.3 Content analysis of the selected topics.

1.4 Writing instructional objectives in behavioural terms.

1.5 Writing pre-requisite knowledge and skills in behavioural terms.

1.6 Developing the criterion tests on the selected topics.

1.7 Evolving the core materials.

STAGE II : WRITING THE PROGRAMMES

This stage consisted of developing programmed learning material on basis of core material. The frames were designed and sequenced by the researcher. The programmes were corrected by the experts and the edited frames were rewritten.

STAGE III : TRY OUT STAGE

The duly edited programmes evolved by the researcher were tried out unit wise as follows :

1) Individual try out : The programmes were administered on five learners in an informal situation, one learner at a time.
2) Small group try out: After making the changes based on individual try out, the programmes were presented to a small but representative group of 10 learners.
3) Final Field try out : This was the final trial of the programme. The entire programme in the final form was administered to a total group of 100 twelfth grade students.

STAGE IV : EVALUATION STAGE

On the basis of the data collected in the final try out, the programmes were evaluated unit - wise in terms of :

1. **Error Rate :** This was calculated on the basis of responses obtainable for each frame. The errors made by

TABLE 6.1 : Analysis of Data

The results obtained from the analysis of data are given below :

Unit No.	*Cumulative Density*	*Error Rate In Percentage*	*Criterion Test Percentage of Errors*	*Criterion Test Percentage of Success*	*Gain Ratio*
PART A : FOOD					
A-1	0.6	2.9	14.5	85.5	.85
A-2	0.6	3.7	12.9	87.1	.87
A-3	0.6	3	8.9	91	.91
A-4	0.6	5.1	10.6	89.4	.89
A-5	0.6	2.8	8.0	92	.92
A-6	0.6	5.6	10.7	89.2	.89
A-7	0.8	5.6	9.2	90.8	.90
PART B : NUTRITION					
B-1	0.6	2.4	10	90	.90
B-2	0.5	2.5	10	90	.90
B-3	0.7	4.8	12.2	87.8	.87
B-4	0.6	4.4	01.8	89.2	.89
B-5	0.7	5.07	14.5	85.5	.85
B-6	0.8	6.8	13.6	86.4	.86
B-7	0.7	6.9	16.9	83.2	.83
B-8	0.7	6.2	17.3	82.7	.82
B-9	0.5	4.2	10.3	89.6	.89
B-10	0.6	4.5	14.4	85.6	.85
B-11	0.7	2.7	12.1	87.9	.87
B-12	0.6	3.6	10.7	89.2	.89
B-13	0.7	6.1	15.6	84.4	.84
B-14	0.7	6.1	9.1	90.9	.90
B-15	0.7	5.8	1.26	87.4	.87
B-16	0.7	2.8	11.3	88.7	.88

Unit No.	*Cumulative Density*	*Error Rate In Percentage*	*Criterion Test Percentage of*		*Gain Ratio*
			Errors	*Success*	
B-17	0.8	4.3	15.7	84.3	.84
B-18	0.8	4.2	15.5	84.5	.84
B-19	0.7	4.2	16	84	.84
B-20	0.7	3.5	12.3	87.8	.87
B-21	0.8	4.4	16.2	83.7	.83
B-22	0.8	3.3	16.07	83.93	.83
B-23	0.8	4.3	14.07	85.3	.85
B-24	0.6	3.7	16.7	83.3	.83
B-25	0.7	4.3	15.3	84.7	.84

individuals on all the responses were counted and added. The error rate in percentage of each programme was then calculated. This data, relating to error rates of the programmes is given in Table 6.1.

2. **Programme Density :** This was another measure to calculate the effectiveness of the programme. The researcher could not measure the difficulty level of a frame without recourse to measurement of the behaviour that the frame called forth. This behaviour was subject to contamination by variables not under control of the researcher. So, the concept of programme density was used to measure the difficulty level of the programme. Independent densities and cumulative density of all the programmes were calculated. This density data is given in Table 6.1.

3. **Sequence Progression :** The programmes were analysed in terms of progression of sequence. Flow charts for all the programmes were drawn and the errors made by individual students were entered. These flow charts helped in locating the errors and in detecting the faulty frames.

4. **Criterion Tests :** In order to ascertain the level of performance of the students obtainable on each unit, criterion tests were administered after the completion of each unit.

Flow charts were prepared on the basis of student's achievements. Gain ratio was calculated on the basis of the criterion tests.

5. **Attitude-Co-eficient :** This was the final measure to help evaluate the effectiveness of the programme. An attitude scale, was developed to calculate the student's attitude towards the programmes. The attitude scale included statements, concerning characteristics of the programme, such as difficulty level, content clarity and language.

DESCRIPTION OF THE MAIN FEATURES OF THE FINAL DRAFT

Thirty two programmes have been evolved for twelfth grade learners studying Home - Science through English medium.

All the programmes have linear format. There are total 1441 frames, out of which 1419 are constructed response type frames and 22 are selection response type frames. The programmed learning materials contain panels, diagrams and tables for illustrating the content.

The programmes start with instruction for the learner and end with criterion test to be completed by the learner. The programmes follow logical sequencing and have been made empirical after three types of trials.

Error rates range between two to seven percent. Programme density ranges between 0.5 to 0.8. Percentage of success ranges between 80% to 92% . The empirically validated data proves that the programmes are quite effective and make the learning of Home-Science easy and interesting.

SUGGESTIONS FOR FURTHER RESEARCH

1. Programmes can be developed for different subjects for XIIth class.
2. Programmes can be developed for different grades of Home Science.
3. Programmes can be developed in different Indian languages, like Hindi, Punjabi.
4. Programmes can be developed for Home Science practicals on mathetical style.
5. CAI - computer assisted instruction can be arranged by preparing the floppies of these programmes.

BIBLIOGRAPHY

Anderson, R.C., and Faust G.W., *Educational Psychology - The Science Of Instruction and Learning.* (New York : Dodd, Mead and Company, 1973.

Austwick, Kenneth (Ed.), *Teaching Machines and Programming.* (New York : Macmmillan Co., 1965)

Barnett Anne, *Food And Nutrition for You* (Hutchinson and Co. Publishers Ltd., 1985).

Best, W.John and Khan, V James, *Research In Education* (Fifth Edition, Prentice Hall of India Private Limited) New Delhi 1986.

Bigge, M.L., *Learning Theories for Teachers,* 4th Ed, Harper and Row, N.Y. 1982.

Bjerstedt, A.K.J.E. *Educational Technology,* (New York : Wiley Interscience, 1972).

Bloom, Benjammin S., et al., *Taxonomy of Educational Objectives - The Classification of Educational Goals Handbook I : The Cognitive Domain.* (New York : Longmans, Green, 1956).

Buch, M. B. (Ed.), *Third Survey of Research in Education.* (National Council of Educational Reasearch and Training, 1978-83).

Callender, Patricia, *Programmed Learning – Its* Development *and Structure.* (London : Longman, Green and Co., 1969).

Davidson Stantley et al., : *Human Nutrition and Dietetics* Sixth Edition (The English Language Book Society and Churchill Livingstone, 1975).

Dececco, John P. (Ed) , *Educational Technology.* (New York : Holt Rinehart and Winston, 1964).

DeCecco, John P., *The Psychology Of Learning And Instruction*. (New York: Prentice Hall Int. Inc., 1968).

Deterline, W.A., *An Introduction to Programmed Instruction.* (New York : Prentice Hall, 1969).

Ebel L. Robert, et. al., *Essentials of Educational Measurement,* Fifth Edition, University of Iowa — (Prentice Hall of India Private Limited, New Delhi, 1991).

Espich, J.E. and Williams B, *Developing Programmed Instructional Materials.* (London : Pitman, 1967).

Fry, Edward B., *Teaching Machines and Programmed Learning,* (New York : Me Graw - Hill, 1963).

Gandhi, Romila and Amarjeet Kaur : *Home Science for Class XII* (Pardeep Publications, Jalandhar 1989) .

Gerras Charles and The Staff of Prevention Magzine. *The Complete Book of Vitamins* (Rodale Press Emmaus P.A. 1977).

Glasser, Robert (Ed.) *Teaching Machines and Programmed Learning. II: Data and Directions.* (Washington, D.C. : National Education Association, 1965).

Green, Edward J., *The Learning Process and Programmed Instruction.* (New York : Holt, Rinehart and Winston, 1962).

Guthrie Andrews Helen, *Introductory Nutrition.* Fourth Edition (The C.V. Mosby Company St. Louis London, Tronto 1979).

Inamdar, J.A. "A study of the effectiveness of the Programmed learning strategy in the subject of Mathematics for Standard VII in relation to some psychology correlates," Ph.D. Edu, Sardar Patel University, 1981.

Jeyachandran, J. "An Experimental Study of the Efficacy of Programmed Filmstrips as a method of teaching History in the Secondary Schools," Ph. D. Edu., M.S. University of Baroda, 1980.

Leith, G.O. et al., A *Handbook of Programmed Learning.* (University of Birmingham, 1966).

Lumsdaine, A.A. and Glaser, R. (Eds.), *Teaching Machines and Programme Learning : A Source Book.* (Washington, D.C. NADAVI, 1960).

Major, R.F., *Preparing Objectives for Programmed Instruction,* (San Frenscisco : Fearon, 1961).

Markle, S.M., *Good Frames and Bad*: A *Grammar of Writing,* (New York: John Wiley and Sons, 1969).

Mavi, N.S., *Programmed Learning: An Empirical Approach,* (Vishal Publications, 1984).

Mavi, N.S., "Development of a Programmed Text in Physical Geography for High School Students", Ph.D., Edu., Kurkeshetra University, 1981.

Osterlind J. Steven : *Constructing Test Items,* University of Missouri Columbia Kluwer Academic Publishers Boston Dordrecht/London. 1989).

Pandey, K.P. *A first Course in Instructional Technology,* (Gaziabad : Amitash Prakashan, Delhi, 1980).

Pandey I.D., "Use of Programmed Instruction on Teaching Mathematics at Primary Level", Ph.D. Edu. Patna University.

Parlikar, K.R., "A Study of Suitability of Programmed Learning in Home - Science Education for Adolescent Girls", Ph.D. Edu, M.S., University of Baroda, 1979.

Pipe, Peter, *Practical Programming* (New York : Holt, Rinehart and Winston, 1965).

Pocztar, Jerry, *The Theory and Practice of* Programmed *Instruction.* (UNESCO, 1965).

Robinson H. Corinne and Lawler R. Marilyn : *Normal and Therapeutic Nutrition.* 16th Edition Oxford and IBH Publishing Co. Pvt. Ltd. 1982.

Rodale J.I. and Staff : *The Complete Book of Minerals For Health.* (Rodale Books, INC Emmaus, PENNA 18049, 1976).

Schramm, Wilbur (Ed.) *The Research of Programmed Instruction.* (Washington, D.C. office of Education, 1964).

Seshadri, M., "An Experiment in the Use of Programmed Instruction In Secondary Schools", Ph.D. Edu., M.S. University of Baroda, 1980.

Shah, J.C., "To Develop and Try Programmed Material in mathematics for Students of Class V in Gujarat State". Ph. D. Edu., Gujrat Vidyapeeth, Ahmedabad, 1981.

Sharma, K. , "A study of a Programme in Classification of Plant Kingdom for High School Students in relation to continuous and Delayed Schedules of Reinforcement", Ph.D. Edu., Himachal Pradesh Univerity, 1981.

Shah G.B. (Ed.) *Studies in Programmed Learning.* (Ananad (W.R.) Charotar Edu. Society 1974).

Smith K.U. and Smith M.F., *Cybernatic Principles of Learning and Educational design.* (New York : Holt, Rinehart and Winston, Inc., 1966).

Smith W.I. and Moore W.J., *Programmed Learning* (New York : Von Nostrand, 1962).

Stolurow et al., *A Guide to Evaluating Self Instructional Programms.* (New York : Holt Rinehert, 1966).

Suthar, K.S., "A study of performance on Programmed Learning Materials in relation to some Psychological Characteristics," Ph.D. Edu., Sardar Patel University, 1981.

Talyzina, Nina, *The Psychology of learning - Theories* of *Learning and Programmed Instructions.* (Moscow : Progress publishers, 1981).

Tolonen, Matti : *Vitamins and Minerals in Health and Nutrition.* (New York, Ellis Horwood, 1990).

Trivedi, I.U., "Use of Banching variety of Programmed Learning Materials as Diagnostic and remedial Tools," Ph. D. Edu., M.S. University of Baroda.

Wilson, Eva D et.al., *Principles of Nutrition,* 4th Edition (John Wiley and Sons New York/Chichester/Brisbanae/ Toronto 1979).

APPENDIX

ATTITUDE SCALE

Dear Student,

The statements given below are designed to find you attitude towards programmed material. Please place a tick mark like (✓) under column 'Yes' if you agree with the statement. If you disagree with a particular statement, put tick mark (✓) under the column "No". If you cannot decide about a statement put a tick mark (✓) under the column "Uncertain".

S. No.	*Statement*	*Yes*	*No*	*Uncer-tain*
1.	Learning through the programmes is easy.	( )	( )	( )
2.	The material which was given in the programmes was clear.	( )	( )	( )
3.	Reading the programmes is easy.	( )	( )	( )
4.	It is difficult to concentrate on the programmes.	( )	( )	( )
5.	While I am reading the programmes my attention gets diverted.	( )	( )	( )
6.	Many things are known by reading the programmes.	( )	( )	( )
7.	The language used in the programmes is easy.	( )	( )	( )

S. No.	*Statement*	*Yes*	*No*	*Uncer-tain*
8.	I can work through the programmes, without taking the help of my teacher or my classmate.	( )	( )	
9.	Home Science lessons become more interesting by studying through the programmes.	( )	( )	( )
10.	I would like to study Home Science through the programmes.	( )	( )	( )
11.	Going through the programmes is very boring.	( )	( )	( )
12.	Unit tests at the end of the programmes are good.	( )	( )	( )
13.	I will never like to study through programmes.	( )	( )	( )